THE TRUTH ABOUT
REPARATIONS AND WAR-DEBTS

THE TRUTH ABOUT
REPARATIONS
AND WAR-DEBTS

BY
THE RIGHT HON. DAVID
LLOYD GEORGE

NEW YORK

Howard Fertig

1970

PRINTED IN THE UNITED STATES OF AMERICA
BY NOBLE OFFSET PRINTERS, INC.

CONTENTS

THE TRUTH ABOUT
REPARATIONS AND WAR-DEBTS

CHAPTER I

INDUSTRIAL depression, far exceeding in extent, persistence and intensity any previous depression within living memory, is widespread throughout the world to-day. It is not confined to one country or group of countries. Severely though we in Great Britain are stricken, we are sharing only the common experience, and many other nations are in far worse plight than ourselves.

Words such as "disaster," "ruin," "catastrophe," had ceased to rouse any sense of genuine apprehension because they had become the commonplaces of political controversy. But they are now finding their way into sober reviews of the state of the world and are charged with a real and terrible meaning. They point to the bankruptcy of great nations, to the desolation of factories, workshops, mines and fields everywhere; to twenty million workers shambling about in enforced idleness with privation and even actual hunger haunting their homes; to Capitalism bewildered and impotent amid the devastation of the industrial and financial system it has set up but failed to control.

The fact of this depression does not need to be demonstrated. Professor T. E. Gregory, reviewing the story of 1931 in the *Manchester Guardian Commercial Annual Review of British Trade*, describes it as a "year of unparalleled economic collapse throughout the world. International trade has been utterly disrupted; the international gold monetary standard has been almost completely abandoned; the central banking

I

system, from which so many great things were expected ten years ago, has been severely strained. . . . It was the year of great depression. It was the most gloomy of the mournful sequence that has filed past since the hectic hopefulness of 1919 and 1920." The *Economist Commercial History and Review of 1931* similarly declares that "In every industry and every country the picture is dismally similar. The story of 1931 is, in fact, a litany of woe and a commination service against increasing misfortune. . . . Although Europe was the centre of the storm, it is possible to search the world outside without finding bright spots." In his Halley Stewart Lecture on February 11th, 1932, Sir Basil Blackett pointed out how, through the financial chaos and collapse of prices throughout the world, we had for the past ten years experienced in heartrending fashion how "every kind of effort towards world recovery and reconstruction, both national and international, had been rendered abortive, often after showing great initial promise of success."

Unemployment in this country has risen to the appalling total of over $2\frac{3}{4}$ millions—this includes the partially unemployed. But we are not the only sufferers in this respect. In Germany, by January 1923, the unemployed numbered over 6 millions—a far higher proportion than ours. In France the unemployed increased sevenfold during 1931, and by January 1932 more than 50 per cent of the workers in French industry and commerce were on short time. The *Times* Paris correspondent, writing on February 12th, 1932, computed that the wholly unemployed in France now numbered $1\frac{1}{4}$ millions, and the partially unemployed $1\frac{3}{4}$ millions. The aggregate is higher than the British figure, and proportionally to industrial population much higher.

The totally unemployed in Italy numbered almost a million by December, in spite of Signor Mussolini's truly heroic efforts to find useful work for all. In the United States of

REPARATIONS AND WAR-DEBTS

America the number at work in manufacturing industries has fallen to less than two-thirds of those employed in 1926. Estimates of the total workless in the States, on a comparable basis to that adopted for their enumeration here (full-time and short-time unemployed lumped together), indicate a figure of round about 12 millions.

Europe is in a bad state, and America is for the time being no better off. What has happened in America is more instructive than the experience of the Old World. A review of the position in the richest country in the world gives a better idea of the depth, extent and origin of the mischief than a survey of the ruin wrought in the war-shattered countries of Europe. In those countries what else could one expect? But America was not long enough in the war, in spite of her prodigious efforts during the last nineteen months of the struggle, to cripple her marvellous resources. The fact that the United States have been hit so hard by world conditions clearly demonstrates that they have found it as impossible to maintain a policy of isolation in peace as they did in war. Three years ago they were scorching along the high road of unexampled prosperity. Exalted authorities promised not only an indefinite continuance of this exhilarating thrill but an acceleration of the speed. It is now rather painful to read extracts from those radiant prophecies. It gives some idea as to how limited is the vision of those who are perched on the highest towers.

If this is the condition of things in a country with the great natural resources, accumulated reserves and wonderful organization of America, we can imagine what must be the problems and the prospects in the overcrowded countries of the Old World. This universal economic blizzard has been sweeping across all countries alike. It has smitten the countries that were victorious in the last war no less than those that were defeated. Countries such as France and the

United States which are swollen with a surfeit of gold are no less stricken than those with an inadequate supply of that metal. Countries which were devastated and exhausted by the war, and countries which on balance profited by the war are alike suffering, and they find that the tale of Midas ought to have taught them that gold is indigestible. It may be all right in the teeth of a nation, but it should not be allowed to travel any further. Countries with high tariff walls are suffering at least as badly as those without. Whatever the cause of the catastrophe, it is clearly something which has devastated the whole economic order of the modern world.

Nor are we left in much doubt as to the nature of the causes that have been at work to produce these distresses. Some of these arise from conditions quite independent of the war, and which were spreading before that catastrophe began. The war only precipitated and aggravated evils in our economic system which were already becoming visible to observant eyes. No permanent remedy is attainable until these evils have been thoroughly diagnosed and skilfully and courageously eradicated. But the war brought evils of its own, which intensified and roused into pernicious activity the mischief lurking in the system. The best-informed leaders in commerce, finance and economics in all countries alike are agreed that there are at least three clear and definite reasons for the dislocation of trade and industry. These are: the mishandling and faulty distribution of the world's gold supplies; the high tariff barriers to international commerce; and the special international indebtedness which is a legacy of the World War.

Amongst the worst of these causes is the gigantic international indebtedness created by the war. It hampers movement, and in the case of one great nation, it threatens to strangle its very life. It curses those who receive as well as those who give. In the following pages I propose to concen-

4

trate upon this issue, and to refer to questions of gold distribution or high tariffs only in so far as they affect it.

What are we to do with War-Debts and Reparations? That is the question which beyond all others has been perplexing the world ever since the World War came to an end.

We have been moving in a vicious circle. Germany has been forced to sell her merchandise abroad on a large scale in order to pay reparations. The creditor countries have been putting up high tariffs in order to protect their own industries against the competition of these goods—the very goods the proceeds from which they are demanding as reparation payments from Germany. A free trade country has a right to expect from other countries the payment of large monetary obligations which they may have incurred to it. But a high tariff country is placing artificial obstacles in the way of the collection of its own book debts. That is why, when the United States demanded payment of the debts due to it from the Allied countries, Britain, France and Italy, these in turn passed the demand on to Germany. Germany made frantic efforts to sell her goods everywhere in order to get the money to pay. But she found the tariff walls against her goods everywhere raised higher and higher. The Hawley-Smoot tariff finally smashed her chances of doing enough business to pay America, and she was driven to default. The British tariff has now destroyed the last hope that she will ever recover as a debt-paying country. The growing difficulties in the way of paying or receiving reparations and war-debts have brought about an embitterment of international relations and an increasing disturbance of international trade, until to-day we are faced with universal depression and stagnation of industry and commerce in debtor and creditor nations alike—a depression which skilled economic and financial investigators assure us is mainly due to this legacy of war liabilities. We have already reached disaster; and ere long

5

disaster may develop into irretrievable ruin of the existing order, if the statesmen of the world do not find courage to grapple with this problem and insist upon a solution of it, however unpalatable that solution may at first seem to some at least of the countries concerned.

To arrive at a wise judgment on the existing problems it might be helpful to recall the facts as to how these debts and indemnities arose, and how they have been dealt with up to the present. Decision should not be obscured by factitious equities and sanctities which have been set up by ignorance, greed, or racial suspicion and hatred as barriers to justice. Seeing that I took an active and leading part alike in the war-time arrangements out of which war-debts arose, and in the peace negotiations which laid the basis for payment of repara-tions, I feel it my duty to lay before my fellow-countrymen a brief summary of a few of the more important historic facts bearing on this issue, including some highly interesting documents and details not previously published, which may help to indicate what is the real foundation of the problem; what was the idea that inspired and guided the framers of the Treaty in respect of reparations; what has been from the outset the attitude of the principal countries concerned towards reparations and debts; and what is the only solution of the acknowledged difficulties which have arisen from these international obligations.

CHAPTER II

THE CASE FOR REPARATIONS

THE World War, prolonged over four years on a more intense and destructive scale than human imagination had ever previously conceived possible, left all the belligerent nations at its close deeply impoverished, burdened with immense debts, and to a greater or less degree exhausted alike in man-power and in material resources, and—most fatal of all—in that nerve-power which enables men to decide promptly and to carry out decisions effectively.

As to the justice of exacting reparations from Germany for the damage caused to other countries by the war, there can be no doubt, once you assume that the German nation was primarily responsible for that war. I am not going to argue the question of war guilt at this stage. It is sufficient for me here to point out that in their dispute with their neighbours, Germany and her ally Austria had their case tried in the Court and by the procedure they themselves had chosen—trial by battle—and lost. It was not the tribunal of our choosing. We had urged a peaceful conference to settle the issues in dispute between Austria and Servia, between the Central Powers and Russia and France. Our overtures were rejected. The rulers of Austria and Germany elected war; and in the arbitrament of war the verdict was given against them. I admit that the decisions of such a court do not settle the merits of the dispute. The worst of war as a method of deciding rights and wrongs is that the verdict too often goes for the strong, and not against the wrong. But

7

the countries that deliberately plunge into that risk cannot complain if it goes against them; for they have chosen the most precarious as well as the most expensive method of procedure because they are better equipped and trained for its rules and intricacies than any of their adversaries. If as losers they have to pay costs, they must not grumble that those costs are heavy. The fees in the courts of War are all on the highest scale.

Had there been an international court in existence in which an action for tort could have been brought against Germany in respect of injuries which other countries had received from her through the war, if the verdict had gone against her, she would legally have been required to pay full damages and all costs of the action. Speaking in the House of Commons in July 1919 on the Versailles Treaty, I pointed out that "if the whole cost of the war, all the costs incurred by every country that has been forced into war by the action of Germany, had been thrown upon Germany, it would have been in accord with every principle of civilized jurisprudence in the world."

Great devastation was wrought in the countries opposed to Germany. In the battlefields of Flanders and the invaded territories of France this devastation was visible to the eye. Here there stretched an expanse, 400 miles long and approximately thirty miles wide of towns, villages, and cultivated land devastated beyond recognition. In our own case the damage was partly visible, in towns bombed or shelled and in millions of tons of mercantile ships sunk. The total bill for damage to our mercantile shipping alone was over £551,000,000. Our more serious devastation was invisible—the shattering of our export trade through our being cut off for over four years from our normal overseas markets. We were the largest international traders in the world and were, therefore, more vulnerable in this respect than any other country. Our

8

customers had been driven either to secure their supplies from rival sources or to start manufacturing for themselves. Indeed, our export trade has never recovered from the war, as the derelict factories of our industrial districts bear melancholy witness. While world trade had by 1927 risen to 120 per cent of the pre-war level, British export trade was only 83 per cent of its pre-war height. That is our real devastated area.

Great liabilities had been incurred by the Allied Powers. In addition to immense internal debts accumulated by all, there were external debts: debts of our Allies to us; debts owed both by them and by us to the United States. These formed part of the cost of beating off what we held to be an attack on civilization and national rights.

There is thus nothing new in the principle of Reparations. It is, as I have already pointed out, no more than an application to communities of the ordinary and accepted principles of law as between individuals. By the civilized law in every land a person who inflicts injury to his neighbour must pay the whole cost, assessed irrespective of his means unless or until he goes bankrupt: when arrangements are made to compound with his creditors on the basis of his marketable assets.

But in preparing the bill for Germany, we did not include all the items which in accordance with equity or traditional practice might have figured there. We had agreed to exact no indemnity, and to confine our claims upon the defeated foe to the cost of making good the damage she had inflicted on the civilian population of the Allies. And while lost trade and war-debts might rationally have been included in those damages, the limits of claim were in fact drawn much more narrowly in the Peace Treaty, to apply only to destruction of material property and to the cost of pensions or other compensations paid to homes

9

shattered by the death or mutilation of their bread-winners. That was the justification and the basis of reparations.

Now comes the question of the extent to which the damage can fairly be collected, having regard not only to the misery this collection in full would bring to the lot of millions of men, women and children in Germany and Austria, but to the wretchedness which the collection has scattered like a pestilence right through every land under the sun. There is the further question, which is becoming more and more obtrusive, of whether a harsh collection does not inflict as much harm on the collectors as on the debtors. The first question is one which is considered by every bankruptcy judge in proceedings for insolvency, and in judgment summons to enforce payment of a debt by instalments. The second question is one which weighs with every wise creditor before he resorts to the extremity of his legal rights. You have two considerations in the enforcement of reparations and international debts: the debtor's capacity to pay without starvation for his family, and the creditor's capacity to receive without ruin to his business.

CHAPTER III

ESTIMATING GERMANY'S CAPACITY TO PAY

The charge is often made that "ignorant politicians" committed the folly of thinking Germany could pay tens of thousands of millions of pounds on account of her reparation debts, and that they enshrined this absurd decision in the Treaty of Versailles.

As a matter of fact, however, in this country it was the politicians who were persistently doubtful as to the possibilities of payment, and the expert authorities who were vivaciously confident. In France the reverse was admittedly the case. I propose to give one or two egregious examples later on of the delusions under which quite eminent French politicians suffered on the subject of Germany's capacity to pay. No protest was raised here from the City as to the fantastic amount of reparations suggested by their foremost authority—indeed, the highest estimate made by anyone at the Peace Conference as to the amount which Germany could pay was made by business men who had the advantage of being advised by a lawyer of brilliant intellect and great judicial experience.

At the end of the war, in 1918, I set up a small committee to investigate this question, in preparation for the Peace Conference. It was appointed not merely in order to guide the Government as to the demand which they could reasonably put forward at the coming conference, but also with a view to obtaining an authoritative report that would damp down the too fierce ardour of an expectant public. The chairman was Mr. W. M. Hughes, Prime Minister of Australia, and the members were the late Mr. Walter Long—a distinguished representative of moderate Conservative opinion; Sir G. E. Foster, the Canadian Finance Minister—a statesman of recognized sanity and moderation and with great experience in public finance; Mr. W. A. S. Hewins, the economist; Lord Cunliffe, the Governor of the Bank of England; and the Hon. Herbert Gibbs, of the firm of Antony Gibbs & Sons. These last two were specially nominated to serve on the Committee as business men of high repute.

It will be seen that this Committee was very far from being dominated by the fire-eating type of politician. Yet in its findings it proposed that the Central Powers should be required to make an annual reparation payment of £1,200,000,000—which figure would, they calculated, represent the interest charges on the whole direct cost of the war to the Allies. It will be seen that on this basis the Germans would have been required to pay within a generation a sum of nearly forty thousand million pounds.

In the light of subsequent events, the findings of this committee make interesting reading. They ran as follows:

"The Committee's Conclusions.

"The conclusions of the Committee may be summarized as follows:

"1. The total cost of the War to the Allies is the measure of the Indemnity which the enemy Powers should in justice pay.

"2. Although it is not yet possible to estimate what the total cost of the War will be, the figures available indicate that so far the direct cost of the War to the Allies has been £24,000,000,000; and the Committee have certainly no reason to suppose that the enemy Powers could not provide £1,200,000,000 per annum as interest on the above amount when normal conditions are restored.

"3. The indemnity should be payable in cash, kind, securities, and by means of a funding loan.

"4. The fear of economic ill-effects to Allied countries from the repayment of the costs of the war is not well founded; whilst without repayment the Allied countries with their man-power seriously reduced, their territory laid waste, their industries paralyzed and burdened with a huge load of debt would be unable to compete successfully in the markets of the world.

"5. The enforcement of an indemnity will operate as a deterrent to future aggression and be a substantial guarantee of the world's peace.

"(Signed)   W. M. HUGHES.

W. H. LONG.

GEO. E. FOSTER.

CUNLIFFE.

HERBERT C. GIBBS.

W. A. S. HEWINS.

G. M. EVANS, Secretary."

To the credit of the British Treasury, I must state that in their view expressed at that moment of triumphant exaltation, £2,000,000,000 was the full measure of the repayments we could possibly expect Germany to make.

The late M. Klotz was M. Clemenceau's Finance Minister, and as such attended discussions on the indemnity question. M. Clemenceau once said of him that he was the only Jew he ever met who knew nothing of finance! After this cruel comment, it will surprise no one to read that M. Klotz held always to the view that Germany must and could pay in full. In the Chamber of Deputies, *"L'Allemagne payera!"* was his answer to every claim and complaint. The late M. Loucheur, on the other hand, was more doubtful. He was indeed one of the shrewdest men I ever met amongst the political figures with whom I had to deal at these International Conferences. If his moral courage had equalled his ability, he would have been a great man. But he always shrank from the thankless and risky duty of telling his countrymen what the true facts were. He knew these facts and frankly admitted them in confidential discussions, but he dared not publish such unpalatable truths.

In 1919 public opinion, both here and in France, was out and out in favour of making Germany pay. Everywhere the people were confronted with unparalleled losses in lives and property. In Britain the capital charge in respect of war pensions alone was estimated at £3,000,000,000. For the immense material damage and expenditure incurred by the Allies in the war, German reparations provided the sole hope of recoupment, and it is not surprising that in estimates of her capacity to pay, the wish sometimes became the father to the thought.

So far as my own view is concerned, it is on record that I never thought Germany could pay these huge sums. Speaking at Bristol on December 11th, 1918, in the course of the election campaign, I said:

"If I were to say to you, not merely that Germany ought to pay, but that we can expect every penny, I should be doing so without giving you the whole of the facts. I consulted our financial advisers. . . . They were doubtful. . . . I have always said we will exact the last penny we can out of Germany up to the limit of her capacity, but I am not going to mislead the public on the question of the capacity until I know more about it, and I certainly am not going to do it in order to win votes. . . . If Germany has a greater capacity, she must pay to the very last penny."

I stood persistently by these two principles: that Germany must pay for the damage she had caused, up to the limit of her capacity; and that we must be prepared to scale down our ultimate demands below the total of what was due, down to the level of what could be paid without inflicting injury on the trade of the recipients.

The view that Germany must be made to pay was held no less definitely by responsible statesmen of all parties in this country. On the day when I made my Bristol speech, Mr. Asquith, addressing the electors of East Fife, said he was in favour of exacting from the wrongdoer the uttermost farthing. The following day, at Pittenween, in reply to the question, "Will you make the Germans pay for the war?" he replied, "Yes, I am in agreement on that matter with what the Prime Minister said yesterday." And on December 13th, asked at Ladybank: "Are you prepared to see that Germany pays to the last halfpenny?" he answered, "I have said so at at least twelve meetings." Similar views were expressed on Labour platforms. Mr. Henderson, speaking at Cardiff on December 7th, 1918, said, "Full indemnity he would support, exacting from Germany the fullest possible restitution for devastation and wrongdoing outside legal warfare. . . . How the Germans should be taxed to meet indemnity it was not our business to dictate. . . ."

Sober financial opinion at the time saw nothing unreasonable in the proposal to exact reparation in full. The *Economist* of December 7th, 1918, while pointing out that the Allied claims on Germany must be in accordance with the terms of the Armistice—i.e., for reparation, not for a war indemnity—contended that Germany could be made to pay:

15

"As for collecting the bill without damaging our industries, this should not be a very difficult matter. Germany, it is true, can only meet the bill that the Allies will present by delivering up ships, plant, securities, gold, and any goods that she can produce in excess of what she needs for subsistence, efficiency, and maintenance of productive power. . . . If she is to pay, that productive power has to be maintained, since it is in goods that the bulk of the payment will have to be made. This means that she will be a keen competitor in all the markets of the world with our products and those of our Allies. So she would have been in any case, and the only effect of her having to pay damages will be that a large part of the profits of her competition will go in enabling us and our Allies to meet part of our war debts. Our war debts raised abroad amount to nearly £1,300,000,000 sterling, and we have sold abroad many hundreds of millions worth of securities which we could gladly replace. If by selling goods Germany is able to pay us in bills of other countries, we shall be able to use them to comfortable advantage. . . ."

In the following April, during the Peace negotiations, Mr. Bonar Law spoke in the House of Commons repeating my warning against cherishing extravagantly high hopes of what could be extracted in payment from Germany. The *Economist* of April 5th, 1919, challenged these doubts. It wrote:

"In normal times, when it is allowed to do business on business methods, Lombard Street has little difficulty in transferring any amount of money between nations that are in economic communication. . . . (Germany's) power to pay is not, as Mr. Bonar Law seemed to think, any the less because before the war she had an adverse balance on visible goods of £70,000,000 a year. We had an adverse balance of about £130,000,000, but we were investing abroad about £200,000,000 a year, according to the usual received estimate. Germany must also have been investing abroad, and any sum that she then had available for investment abroad she can, if her industry is able to grow to its old figures, put into meeting the debt to her creditors on war account. As her industry expands that power will increase."

These quotations sufficiently illustrate and support my claim that economic authority was far more confident than were the politicians that reparations could be paid. As to the question whether our claim on Germany was to be for an indemnity or only for reparations, i.e., a penal fine which the victors exact from their defeated foe, or simply a bill for civil damages suffered by their people, it had soon grown obvious to me that Germany's capacity to pay would be exhausted before the bill for reparations alone had been fully met, so that the question whether what we received from her should be classed as an indemnity or a reparation payment became a matter of purely academic interest. But the inclusion in our reparation claim of a rough assessment of the annual pecuniary charge in respect of our heavy casualty list affected the proportions of the reparation account presented by the Allied countries respectively. Our own representatives on the Reparation Committee at the Conference were Mr. W. M. Hughes, Lord Cunliffe, and Lord Sumner. I placed Lord Sumner on this committee because as a judge of great distinction, capacity and experience, he could bring to bear on this difficult question a judicially moderate view. Lord Cunliffe, coming from the Bank of England with a wide experience of business and high finance, made himself responsible for the highest estimate given by anyone of Germany's capacity to pay, which he put at £24,000,000,000. If Lord Sumner disagreed I have no recollection of receiving from him any note of dissent. I am not aware that any leading British, French or American authority in financial or economic circles at that time seriously challenged the proposition that very large sums could be obtained from Germany, except Mr. J. M. Keynes. M. Tardieu reveals in his book, *The Truth About the Treaty*, that the American experts considered the following as the maximum payments possible:

Payments before 1921	20,000,000,000 gold marks.
Payments from 1922 to 1931	60,000,000,000 " "
Payments from 1932 to 1941	80,000,000,000 " "
Payments from 1942 to 1951	100,000,000,000 " "
	260,000,000,000

or say, £13,000,000,000.
The total of these payments, allowing for interest, represented at current rates a present value of 140,000,000,000 gold marks.

M. Tardieu admits that at Versailles I was opposed to these large estimates, and records that I declared in regard to them: "We are going to throw Germany into the arms of the Bolsheviks. Besides, for her to pay the sum which we have in mind, and which it is just she should pay, she would have to occupy a still greater place in the markets than before the war. Is that to our interest?"

I have no recollection of ever having heard M. Clemenceau express any opinion on the amount of German reparations, or the capacity of Germany to pay. He generally listened to all the discussions without himself expressing any definite conclusion.

Mr. Keynes, examining the question in his *Economic Consequences of the Peace*, came to the conclusion that £2,000,000,000 was an outside figure, and would probably prove excessive.

For this estimate M. Tardieu denounces him as "the pro-German scribe from Cambridge," and states that his estimate "oversteps the limits of permissible tomfoolery, and is only making fun of Germany's victims." I wonder whether M. Tardieu is still of the same opinion. If he is, it bodes ill for any settlement at the Lausanne Conference.

CHAPTER IV

It was not found possible at Versailles to compute with anything like accuracy the total bill which should be presented to Germany on behalf of the Allied and Associated Powers for repairing the damages suffered by them, even in terms of the limited schedule of items to which reparation claims were restricted.

For example, the French claims were at the outset of a most extravagant character. When M. Loucheur brought in his first bill for damages, he estimated the cost of reconstruction of the devastated regions in North-East France at 75,000,000,000 francs (£3,000,000,000). I was staggered at the amount, and asked him at what figure the total wealth of France at the outbreak of war was estimated; and when this was supplied, I found that the entire house property of France was valued in the *Annuaire Statistique de la France*, 1917, at only 59,500,000,000 francs, or far less than he proposed to charge for reconstruction of the war zone alone; and be it remembered that the area of substantial devastation was only about 4 per cent of the total area of France. M. Klotz, the French Minister of Finance, subsequently went further still, and estimated the total damage to French property— exclusive of reparation claims for pensions and allowances— at 134,000,000,000 francs, or £5,360,000,000!

Admittedly one of the difficulties in estimating the bill for reconstructing the devastated areas was the greatly increased cost of building immediately after the war. Not only had normal building costs risen, but the standard of housing and of factory construction was also much higher than it was when the destroyed structures and their equipment were first set up. Building costs have since then fallen to little more than half their immediate post-war level, and actual reconstruction costs will to this extent have fallen below initial estimates. But the improved standard of construction has been maintained.

In comparing the actual expenditure which has since that time been incurred in repairing the damage received by France during the war, with the foregoing estimates, it must be borne in mind that in the interval the French franc has been inflated and devalued, and ultimately stabilized at one-fifth its former value. Making this allowance, we find that whereas M. Loucheur's estimate was £3,000,000,000, and that of M. Klotz £5,360,000,000, the 1928 report of Mr. J. R. Cahill, Commercial Counsellor to the British Embassy in Paris (when reconstruction was practically complete), shows the total estimated expenditure for restoration of France's devastated areas and war damages compensation as £859,000,000 (106.5 milliards of francs, converted at par of exchange).*

Further, the reconstruction has done very much more than make good the damage wrought by the war. It has given to the ruined departments a most up-to-date and efficient equipment, as regards both housing and industry. Mr. Cahill's report states that "the devastated areas possess now an economic capacity far superior to that of 1914. Their

*According to an official French statement, published in *Le Temps* of 13th February, 1932, the actual sums expended to date by France in repair of war damages total 103 milliards of francs (£830 million at par of exchange). The statement adds that reckoning gold values of the payments at the times they were made, their value in present-day francs would be 175 milliards; but it must be pointed out that whatever the gold value of the franc at the time France raised the loans out of which she financed restoration of her devastated areas, the investors are now only being paid in depreciated francs, so that the larger figure is misleading.

coal mines produced in 1927 33,320,000 tons against 27,390,000 in 1913, their coke ovens 3,280,000 as against 2,460,000, and in patent fuel 2,420,000 against 1,800,000 tons; in gas, benzol, synthetic ammonia and other by-products the advance has been in a far greater proportion. In equipment, whether as regards permanent plant, electricity installation, mechanical appliances for coal-getting and transport, the advance has been immense." He reports a great increase in the output of iron mines and in the efficiency of iron and steel works. "Eighteen large works with 86 blast furnaces which were completely wrecked have been reconstructed with the most modern power houses, coke oven batteries with recovery of by-products, converters, rolling mills." The same is true of the textile industries of the area, where all losses have been made good by the newest types of machinery in practically all cases, and when rebuilding was requisite by better planned, better equipped, and larger units. "Similar reconstruction and superior capacity are to be observed as regards the very numerous small breweries, brickworks, distilleries, buildings and other undertakings in these areas. . . . Owing to the nature of the reconstruction one may regard the industrial reconstruction from the point of view of potential production as more than completed, and may even assume an excess margin of, say, 25 to 40 per cent."

"Almost a revolution has been effected in housing conditions . . . a great improvement has taken place in the type of dwelling; in place of the old normal type of rows of small (often back-to-back) houses known as *corons*, the new buildings are very often detached houses with two to four dwellings, and many are semi-detached houses; most have running water, electricity, douches and other modern conveniences indoors; and a relative abundance of garden or allotment space is provided."

REPARATIONS AND WAR-DEBTS

The report notes a similar improvement in the quality of the public services. Roads, bridges, railways, stations, electricity and gas supply are all far in advance of the pre-war level. The immense increase of riches in these departments of France resulting from the quality of reconstruction work carried out in them is shown by the fact that whereas before the war the State used to draw about 16 or 17 per cent of its taxation revenue from these ten counties, in 1925 it drew 19 per cent and in 1926, 22 per cent of its revenue from them.

In the light of this report, it is clear that a figure considerably less than the £860,000,000 actually expended on compensation and reconstruction of the devastated areas would represent the real cost of making good to its pre-war standard the damaged property of France. For this, £650,000,000 would probably be an outside figure as compared with the £5,360,000,000 claimed by M. Klotz in 1919. This illustrates the difficulty with which we were faced at the Peace Conference in attempting to estimate the Bill for Reparations.

It is always assumed by those who have never read the Treaty of Versailles, that this much-abused and little-perused document fixed a fabulous indemnity for payment by Germany. It did nothing of the kind. The Treaty may have its defects, but this is not one of them, for it fixed no sum for payment, great or small. Before people rush to criticize the Treaty of Versailles they should do, not the authors but themselves the justice of at least perusing its actual terms, instead of satisfying themselves with reading or listening to hostile and ill-informed perversions of its contents. The reparation clauses cover *two* pages and no more; is it too great a strain on high-minded readers to ask them to read these pages before they condemn?

The total of the Bill for Reparations was not then known, nor the debtor's capacity. Accordingly, no sum was inserted in the Treaty, assessing either the total liability of Germany or the amounts she would be required to pay yearly in liquidation of her debt. Instead of this, it was stipulated that a reparation commission should be set up to assess the damage and decide how much Germany could pay, and in what instalments. It was in effect stipulated that the payment exacted should not necessarily be the amount of the damage but the proportion of it Germany was capable of paying. On these questions, Germany was given the right to be heard before adjudication. By unanimous agreement of the Powers represented on the Commission, any part of Germany's liability for reparations might be cancelled.

To make this point clear, I give the relevant clauses of the Treaty of Versailles:

"Article 233.

"The amount of the above damage for which compensation is to be made by Germany shall be determined by an inter-Allied commission, to be called the *Reparation Commission*, and constituted in the form and with the powers set forth hereunder and in Annexes II to VII inclusive hereto.

"This Commission shall consider the claims and give to the German Government a just opportunity to be heard.

"The findings of the Commission as to the amount of damage defined as above shall be concluded and notified to the German Government on or before May, 1921, as representing the extent of that government's obligations.

"The Commission shall concurrently draw up a schedule of payments prescribing the time and manner for securing and discharging the entire obligation within a period of thirty years from May 1, 1921. If, however, within the period mentioned Germany fails to discharge her obligations, any balance remaining unpaid may, within the discretion of the Commission, be postponed for settlement in subsequent years, or may be handled otherwise, in such manner as the

Allied and Associated Governments, acting in accordance with the procedure laid down in this part of the present Treaty, shall determine.

"Article 234.

"The Reparation Commission shall after May 1, 1921, from time to time, *consider the resources and capacity of Germany, and after giving her representatives a just opportunity to be heard, shall have discretion to extend the date, and to modify the form of payments, such as are to be provided for in accordance with Article 233; but not to cancel any part, except with the specific authority of the several governments represented upon the Commission."*

It will be seen that these two articles, particularly the second of them, permit a wide elasticity in the arrangements made for reparation payments; (1) they give Germany a right of appeal from time to time to the Commission on the question of capacity; (2) they also give her a right to be heard on that appeal; (3) they give the Commissioners discretion to modify the payments; and (4) they even envisage the possibility, by unanimous agreement of the governments concerned, of cancellation up to any extent of Germany's total liability. There are multitudes who treat every alteration effected in the annuities which were originally fixed for Reparation payments, as if it were a departure—to the detriment of the victors—from the consecrated terms of the Treaty of Versailles; whereas in fact the provisions of the Treaty incorporate machinery designed for the express purpose of enabling such modifications to be made from time to time without involving any change in the Treaty for their ratification.

There has undoubtedly been one departure from the terms of the reparation sections of the Treaty—a fundamental departure. It has, however, been entirely to the detriment of the vanquished. From this, the whole trouble has arisen.

REPARATIONS AND WAR-DEBTS

The Treaty provided that the body to be set up for deciding the amount to be paid in respect of reparations should be composed of a representative each from the United States of America, the British Empire, France, Italy and Belgium. With the exception of the U.S.A., all these Powers are pecuniarily interested in the verdict. At best it was therefore on the face of it not a very impartial tribunal. Still, Britain, as a great world trading community, being more interested in a settlement than in a few millions more or less of indemnity wrung out of Germany, the presence of the United States and Britain together on the Commission constituted a guarantee for moderation of judgment.

But as a result of the refusal of the United States to ratify the Treaty of Versailles, the only completely disinterested party was withdrawn from the tribunal. As a result the most interested party is in the chair, with a casting vote. That was not the treaty signed by Germany.

If you sign an agreement to pay a sum to be awarded by A, B, C, D, and E, trusting for a fair hearing largely to the influence of A, who is not only very powerful but completely disinterested, and A then retires from the Board of Arbitrators, you are entitled to claim that the character of the agreement is changed, and that it no longer holds good.

The withdrawal of America from the Commission—after Germany had already signed the Treaty—completely changed the balance and therefore the character of this tribunal. No person whose sense of justice was not drenched in prejudice could pretend that in its mutilated form it was either impartial in its composition or judicial in its methods.

Unfortunately with reference to the Treaty of Versailles a school of interpretation has arisen which seems to maintain that the ordinary precepts of fair play do not apply to Clauses that affect the vanquished. I could furnish many examples of this unscrupulous attitude taken on reparations and dis-

26

armament. It is not a question of compassionate treatment of the vanquished, but of giving them stern fair play. It is not a question of straining the quality of mercy, but whether we are to be called upon to strain the quality of justice. The representatives of France and Belgium on the Reparation Commission have been able and honourable men, anxious to do justice; but they have had behind them a vigilant, jealous and exacting opinion, constantly ready to overpower their judgment. It is not the opinion of the French or Belgian peasants and workmen. Their chief desire is peace—and injustice is the deadly foe of peace. But they are too occupied with the ordinary avocations of a hard-working people to give much thought to the intricacies or the implications of the "policy of enforcement." The result is that the interpretations of the Treaty have been influenced by a small but bustling metropolitan coterie who never in their hearts made peace with Germany. Unlike our own representative, the French and Belgian representatives on the Commission have been firmly controlled by their governments, which in turn were largely swayed by the press of this aggressive clique. They were forced into the rôle of mere delegates, compelled to wrest their own better informed judgment on the issues confronting them in obedience to the orders issued to them from behind. M. Poincaré did not attempt to conceal the fact that the French Government issued its orders to its representative on that "judicial" body. On various occasions the result has been that France and Belgium have on the Commission often worked in concert to urge the extremer view, while Italy has, on the whole, agreed with Great Britain in counselling moderation; but France in the chair has had the casting vote. The British Empire have been generally represented on the Commission by a financial expert. On the other hand, the leading French delegate who is also chairman of the Commission has for the most part been a prominent politician drawn from the section which thought the Treaty too mild in its treatment of Germany. M. Poincaré held that position for some time. M. Barthou has now occupied the chair for years.

It has thus been found necessary to go outside the Treaty of Versailles when dealing with reparations, in order to bring America in again, and thus restore the original scheme. The Dawes Commission, which straightened out matters temporarily after France had plunged into the tragic folly of the Ruhr invasion, and furnished a basis for the resumption of reparation payments, and more recently the Young Plan, which made the latest settlement, were both inside the four corners of the original treaty plan, but outside what was left of the Treaty after America's refusal to ratify. Each of these plans superseded the mutilated Reparation Commission by an arrangement which made possible the co-operation of the non-ratifying Power, the United States, in aiding with her disinterested counsel the settlement of the terms for Germany's payments. In fact, however, this was a reversion to the machinery which the Treaty had originally contemplated.

When the Peace Treaty was being drafted, the American delegation in particular were strongly in favour of inserting precise figures defining the amount of Germany's total liability and the rate at which she should be required to discharge it. In the light of after-events, I can only feel profoundly thankful that I held out stubbornly against this proposal. At that time the raging passions of the war had not subsided and little was known of the difficulties of payment of large sums, and any effort to fix a definite sum would have landed us in a grotesque figure. The lowest figure suggested by even a United States financial expert was £3,000,000,000. The inevitable compromise would have reached higher altitudes of impracticability.

Had we attempted to insert a figure which would approximate to what is now recognized by the most relentless reparationist as Germany's real capacity to pay, French and Italian, and even British opinion would have been at that time so bitterly hostile, that the Treaty could never have been carried; for whilst France would have been satisfied with nothing which did not in effect enable the whole damage inflicted by the war to the furthest limit to be laid on Germany's back—they would have angrily refused to contemplate anything less—Britain and Italy were also smarting from their wounds and were therefore almost as irritated with those who inflicted them (Britain was specially exasperated by the savage callousness of the submarine attacks on our sailors); and they were also convinced that Germany was quite capable of paying stupendous sums by way of reparation.

On the other hand, even had we succeeded in getting the most moderate figure then contemplated inserted in the Treaty, we should still have assessed Germany's liabilities at a level which events have proved to be much above her capacity to pay; and any future attempt to modify the bill would have been met with the outcry that we were tampering with the sanctity of the Treaty. Nobody knew better than M. Clemenceau how intractable French opinion was at that date. He therefore readily assented to any procedure which would necessitate a postponement of any immediate attempt to fix the figure of reparations.

I maintain that in face of these facts the framers of the Treaty took the wise course in arranging a long delay before the first tentative figure was reached of the total liability, as well as of the amount to be exacted, and providing that even afterwards, Germany could appeal from time to time against that or any subsequent figure on the ground of incapacity to pay. The elasticity of the Treaty clauses had made it possible for the Allied demands on Germany to be adjusted by the cooler light of reason and of practical experience, rather than stereotyped amid the hot passions and post-war bitterness of 1919. Reports of the many post-war conferences held to discuss reparations show that even by May 1921—the date fixed for delivery of the bill for damages—the lava had not cooled.

It is noteworthy that each of the subsequent conferences has reduced the demands upon Germany below the level at which they had previously been fixed.

In illustration of this, it may be convenient here to set out in summary fashion the progressive modifications which have been made in the Bill, as regards both the total and the yearly instalments demanded. They can be tabulated as follows:

Boulogne Conference, June 20th, 1920.

Yearly payments demanded from Germany:

1921-26	..	3,000,000,000	gold marks per annum.
1926-31	..	6,000,000,000	" " " "
1931-63	..	7,000,000,000	" " " "

making a total payment of 269,000,000,000 gold marks.

Paris Conference, January 29th, 1921.

The French Finance Minister opened this Conference by going back on the Boulogne figures, and demanding that the German annuity should be assessed at 12,000,000,000 gold marks for 42 years. After days of discussion the yearly payments demanded from Germany were fixed as follows:

1921-23	..	2,000,000,000	gold marks per annum.
1923-26	..	3,000,000,000	" " " "
1926-29	..	4,000,000,000	" " " "
1929-32	..	5,000,000,000	" " " "
1932-63	..	6,000,000,000	" " " "

making a total payment of 226,000,000,000 gold marks, in

addition to which there was to be a levy of 12 per cent of the value of German exports throughout the 42 years.

German Offer (via the U.S.A.), April 24th, 1921.
Capital liability—50,000,000,000 gold marks, paid off with interest by instalments totalling 200,000,000,000 gold marks.

Reparation Commission Announcement, April 27th, 1921.
Capital liability—132,000,000,000 gold marks, to be settled by an issue of bonds. Germany to pay 2,000,000,000 gold marks per annum, plus 26 per cent of the value of German exports.

Dawes Plan, April 11th, 1924.
Yearly payments demanded from Germany:

1924-25	..	1,000,000,000 gold marks per annum.
1925-26	..	1,220,000,000 " " " "
1926-27	..	1,200,000,000 " " " "
1927-28	..	1,750,000,000 " " " "
1928-29	..	2,500,000,000 " " " "

and subsequently at this last annual rate. The duration of the payments was not fixed by the Dawes Committee, but left to be settled afterwards.

Young Plan, June 7th, 1929.
Yearly payments demanded from Germany to be spread over 60 years, slowly increasing in amount up to 1966, the average prior to that year being 1,989,000,000 gold marks per annum, and thereafter diminishing till the end of the period.

Of these sums, 660,000,000 marks a year were to be payable unconditionally, but postponement up to two years at a time could be arranged for the balance due in any year.

REPARATIONS AND WAR-DEBTS

These figures show how the annual payments demanded from Germany were successively scaled down from 7,000,000,000 gold marks a year in 1920 to an average of less than 2,000,000,000 in 1929.

At the same time, it must be pointed out that none of these modifications involves any departure from the terms of the Treaty of Versailles; and in fact, only the last-named, the Young Plan, implies any reduction of the claims on Germany below the total liability fixed in 1921 by the Reparation Commission, and this was agreed to unanimously by all the Powers, and was therefore within the terms of the Treaty. The Dawes Plan, it is true, had fixed an annual rate of payment insufficient even to meet normal interest charges on the principal sum owing, but had left open the possibility, not only of continuing these payments indefinitely, but of readjusting them at some later date. The Young Plan cut down the liability by fixing a limited term for the reduced payments it proposed. But we have seen that such a partial cancellation by agreement of the interested Powers was provided for in the Treaty.

CHAPTER V

FRENCH AND BRITISH VIEWS ON THE PROBLEM

AT THIS stage in the narrative I do not think I can do better than insert a rather full account of the discussion which took place in January 1921, just nineteen months after the Treaty of Versailles was framed, at an allied conference in Paris.

This discussion vividly illustrates the views which were taken in those early days by France and by Britain respectively as to the capacity of Germany to pay reparations, and as to the nature of the problem which those payments presented to the creditor countries. It is particularly interesting to us to-day, because it furnishes a remarkably clear statement of the French position—lucid, logical, persuasive, yet curiously unaware of obvious economic facts; and at the same time it shows that so long ago as January 1921 the British, while warmly sympathizing with the needs and difficulties of their Allies, were under no illusion about the realities of the problem, and particularly about the limitations which hedged the payments of reparations.

This conference was held in Paris, on January 24th-29th, 1921. The view of French statesmanship as to the reparations which could and should be required from Germany was stated by M. Doumer, now the President of the French Republic. He was then Finance Minister in M. Briand's administration. A cultured man, of solid rather than brilliant qualities, he is an attractive speaker, an able and experienced administrator, whose outlook represents that of the average middle-class Frenchman. M. Doumer's unblemished integrity, his honourable career, and the terrible sacrifice he was called upon to make for his country in the Great War—the greatest sacrifice a devoted parent can be called upon to face —all had won for him by 1921 the respect of Frenchmen of all classes. His charm of manner—a charm arising out of a kindly and genial nature—added popularity to respect. The fact that he has just recently been elected to the Presidency against so formidable a rival as M. Briand shows the confidence and affection he has aroused amongst his compatriots. It may be taken for granted that he is generally acknowledged to belong to that type of calm and temperate politician who shuns extreme views on all questions but has not achieved much in the settlement of any question. That is the favourite timber out of which the Third Republic carves its presidents. M. Clemenceau at the height of his popularity was thrown over for M. Deschanel. M. Briand at the climax of his great fame was discarded in favour of M. Doumer. Therefore when I quote M. Doumer's speech it may be safely assumed that I am not culling posies from the wild flowers of Chauvinist meadows.

On the third day of this Paris conference, M. Briand called upon his Finance Minister "to place before the Allies in conference assembled the considered views of France and her leaders on reparations and more especially on the amount Germany should and could pay." After an eloquent passage about the undoubted damage and suffering inflicted on France M. Doumer proceeded to remind the conference of the financial burden that was being carried by the Allied countries which had been victims of German aggression, really because Germany had, up to the moment, *paid no reparation*. (She had then paid over twice as much as the huge indemnity paid by France in 1871!) He continued:

"On the method of fixation of the sum to be paid, there

seems to be little doubt; it is the sum which would represent the present cost of repairing the damages done by our late enemy. I think that an estimate of these damages is possible. Great Britain, France, Italy, and the other Allies are all able to establish, with sufficient approximation, the total amount of reparation damages which are due from Germany. . . .

". . . France has made her calculations on the basis of gold, and has taken the valuation of the material damage sustained on the basis of its value in 1914. France has then tried to ascertain what would be the index number to be applied in order to harmonize this 1914 valuation with the increased cost of materials and cost of living which has since taken place. If one examined the subject a little more deeply, it was easy to observe after all that the rise in prices was in direct ratio with the fall in the exchange value of the franc. . . .

". . . The figure which I have to suggest may seem enormous, but it must be borne in mind that this is the total sum of reparation. The figure for France is estimated at 110 milliard gold marks" (£5,500,000,000).

I asked M. Doumer whether this was the total claim of France, and he replied that it was the total of the French claims in capital. He proceeded:

"I am convinced that this sum would not cover all the actual expenses that France would be called upon to pay under the heading of reparation and I think that this remark would also apply in the case of Great Britain, Italy and Belgium. I think that France would probably have to spend as much as 120 to 130 milliard gold marks. At any rate, I am quite certain—and I have a certain amount of experience on this question, both in Parliament and in other quarters—that this figure of 110 milliards* would be below what they would actually have to disburse" . . .

He then proceeded to add up British, Italian and Belgian claims and concluded:

"Therefore, the whole of the German debt to the Allies figured out on this basis would amount approximately to the sum of 212 milliard gold marks. . . . For purposes of *convenience* they would put the amount down as 200 milliard gold marks" (£10,000,000,000).

He reckoned that the interest on the amount would come to £500,000,000 and that 1 per cent Sinking Fund would liquidate the capital liability in 42 years. The annuity paid by Germany would thus be £600,000,000 for 42 years. (12 milliard gold marks.)

Continuing he said:

"I am aware that the Treaty has laid down that the Allies should consider Germany's capacity to pay. My conviction is that Germany could bear this burden. If Germany could not do so, I wonder how France could hold her own in the same circumstances. If Germany, which is a country with double the population of France, with her industries practically intact, could not find 12 milliard gold marks per annum, in what situation would France find herself? Of course there is the possible risk of bankruptcy in Germany and it may be said that Germany may be led to ruin, but if any bankruptcy is to take place, I do not think it is fair that it should be France that should incur such bankruptcy in order that Germany should escape paying this 12 milliard per annum

---

*The actual disbursement on reparations account by France has been Fr. 103 milliards, or say 17 milliard gold marks.

for the war. The economic capacity of Germany is being restored. . . .

". . . What would be the position of a private individual in such a case? Such a person had either to pay his debt or go bankrupt. What the private individual had to do was to set aside part of his capital or endeavour to undertake some sort of credit operation which would be practically equivalent. Germany could do that."

He then proceeded to explain how Germany could pay this enormous annuity.

"She has State property to an extent which no other nation of Europe possesses. France has no State mines and no State coalfields as Germany has; Great Britain has not either, and I am not aware that Belgium or Italy has. Germany has what are called fiscal mines. It is quite possible for her to live without these fiscal mines, and she could hand over this property to a company, or in any other form that might be evolved. Germany possesses the whole of the railway systems; France only possesses part. I am not aware that Great Britain possesses any State railways at all. If therefore Germany says that she cannot pay, let her alienate part of her own State property which is not absolutely essential to her national life. There are many countries which manage to carry on without State railways. Then, again, she has enormous forests. Germany therefore actually has the assets which she could simply set aside out of her capital in order to meet her obligations even in the first year. I am inclined to say that it is her business to do so. She has accepted the debt; she has signed the Treaty of Versailles because she found at the time an advantage in so doing; because she did not know that she would not be otherwise confronted with worse conditions. She must now meet those obligations, and what

37

would urge her to do so would be to impose penalties if they were not carried out. This has happened before in the case of other countries, which have had to live up to their engagements. Commissions have been set up, for instance, in Turkey and in other countries, in order to collect revenue through customs and other sources. This sort of sanction is rather a painful one which it would, of course, be better to avoid, but if such a penalty were hung over the head of Germany she would feel it incumbent upon her to do everything she could to meet her obligations to pay what the Allies wished her to pay. . . .

". . . But at any rate Germany must pay, and pay now, because the Allies cannot wait any longer. France is practically at the end of her resources. The Allies have been paying on account of Germany ever since the Armistice, and France has set aside, for purposes of reparations, 40 *milliard francs*. . . ."

M. Doumer, continuing, said in conclusion:

"I would like to make three important suggestions:

"Firstly, I suggest that they should decide that by May 1st, 1921, within the limits established by the Treaty, the Allies should draw up as exactly as possible the total indebtedness of Germany in regard to reparations.

"Secondly, that the Allies should notify Germany under what conditions, and in what manner, she can pay—whether or not it would be advisable to have an immediate settlement by the issue of negotiable bonds, covering external debt, with penalties provided for.

"Thirdly, as regards sanctions, all I wish to say is that I have no wish to recommence war. . . . Ten classes have been mobilized during the war, and they have now disappeared. . . . If Germany knew that certain sanctions would be imposed upon her in case of non-fulfilment, I think that she would make the necessary endeavours in order to meet her obligations."

I think everyone will agree that this was a most remarkable speech. So remarkable, indeed, did it appear to me that I asked M. Doumer to let me postpone my reply to it until the following day. Meantime, I asked if I might put to him just a few questions—not in any controversial sense—in order to make it quite clear what was the exact nature of his proposals.

I reproduce in dialogue form the substance of the discussion which then ensued:

MR. LLOYD GEORGE: There was one part of M. Doumer's speech which will not require examination by the British Delegation, because we are in such complete accord, and that was the moral obligation of Germany to pay damage for the terrible injury which she so wantonly inflicted primarily upon France. I want to emphasize that France has undoubtedly been the greatest sufferer, although Belgium and Great Britain have also suffered. That particular part of M. Doumer's speech does not require a moment's postponement to answer, because as I have already said, I agree with every sentiment which M. Doumer has expressed. It is only when I come to the question of ways and means of enforcing that moral obligation upon Germany that I feel any doubt and I would, therefore, like to have a further examination. . . .

. . . . I would like to ask M. Doumer whether he feels confident that Germany could pay 12 milliard gold marks per annum outside her frontier—in France, in Italy, in Great Britain and in Belgium? I wish to know how those 12 milliard gold marks are to be paid by Germany; obviously it is no good sending 12 milliard paper marks to be transferred from Germany, to France, or to Great Britain, or to Italy, or to the rest of the Allies? That is the question that perplexes me, and if M. Doumer has a scheme which would enable that to be done it would be a most invaluable contribution to the solution of our difficulties.

M. DOUMER: I have no scheme at the moment, because I do not expect that the Allies will impose their decisions by force, or that we intend to settle ourselves the economic life of Germany. . . .

. . . The question is, how can she pay out these 12 milliard gold marks? I am aware that she could not do this probably in the first year. At the beginning she would probably have to take a certain sum out of her capital in order to make good the interest due to the Allies—she would have to accept mortgages on her mines or on her railway systems, or by participation in business enterprises. That would be for the first year, but after that the fact is that she must produce enough in order to be able to balance her trade and the revenue which she may be drawing from abroad, so that she may be able to have in gold or goods the necessary assets. Goods exported are equivalent to gold. Before the war Germany, as everyone knows, had a considerable trade and I think that British industries as well as French industries have reason to remember this. How can Germany settle this balance? I do not wish to appear pedantic, but the answer is by balancing foreign trade—to balance the assets and the liabilities. Germany must adjust her affairs in such a way that the figures of her export trade are above those of her import trade; to do this she must work. It would be too easy if after letting hell loose upon the world she had nothing more to do than before the war. Germany must be able by her own work to produce enough to pay her debts and the difference must be equivalent to 12 milliard gold marks. As long as her external revenue does not bring in sufficient money she will have to find that sum from elsewhere. Up to that time what will she do? *Well, she can borrow.* France cannot balance her exports and imports and she is bound to borrow and Germany must do the same. I am told that the balance of trade is improving and that Germany has now been able to reach a proper equilibrium between her exports and imports and in the very near future her productive capacity will still further be increased. Either Germany will have to pay or we, the Allies, will have to pay, and after all it is for Germany to pay her own debts.

MR. LLOYD GEORGE: I am afraid that I do not even now quite follow what is in M. Doumer's mind. Before the war the total of Germany's export was 10 milliards of gold marks. Her imports were very nearly 11 milliards. She had to use her exports to pay for the raw material that enabled her to produce goods for export—cotton, wool, rubber, etc.—and she had to get a certain amount of food from outside. If the whole of her exports were paid over to France and the rest of the Allies she would not be able to buy the raw material which would enable her to export. Germany cannot pay in gold—she has not enough gold to pay one-tenth of these 12 milliard marks. Therefore, she has to pay in goods or in services; she has, however, also to pay for her raw material and for her food. The question I would like to ask M. Doumer is, where are the 12 milliard gold marks to come from? I have been on the look-out for them now for a couple of years and if I could only get someone to point them out to me I should be very glad; but they are certainly not in Germany's exports. Germany exported 10 milliards at a time when she was able to trade with Russia and Austria and Central Europe, and when that part of the world was in a position to pay.

M. DOUMER: I must point out that the value of 12 milliard gold marks to-day is no longer what it was before the war, because the purchasing power of gold is no longer the same. If we take the figure arrived at at Spa—the figure of 2—if we divide 12 milliard by 2 we get 6 milliard, and if we take the more moderate figure of 1.70 the figure arrived at is actually 7 milliard gold marks.

The problem confronting Germany is, therefore, that of making her exports exceed her imports by 7 milliards, and it is not insoluble. A man with an annual income of £20,000 and a liability of £12,000 is obliged by the nature of things to live on £8,000 a year. Germany is in a position to make up whatever deficit exists between her trade balance and the seven milliards demanded by restrictions on imports. . . .

When we consider Germany's position before the war, she may have been able to afford an import surplus. In those days she imported certain things because she thought she could afford them; but there were certain commodities which she was not obliged to buy. Before the war, Germany did not import only raw materials and her necessary foodstuffs, but she imported manufactured articles and other things. She may say that she is unable to pay, but nevertheless she can diminish her expenses. I am aware of the argument, of course, in regard to the increase of wages, but this is an expense shared by us all. Everyone is aware that the cost of living and prices generally have gone up, and therefore these 12 milliards of gold marks in reality represent only half that value. In view of the fact that Germany still has a large amount of capital with her plant and machinery practically untouched, and 60.7 million inhabitants—that is to say, more than double the population of France even at the time France mobilized her men between the ages of 20 and 45 (France mobilized 7,000,000 men during the war, and during this time the birth rate was very low)—I think 12 milliards is a low figure. I quite agree that an enquiry should be made into Germany's capacity to pay. If she does not pay, then we shall have to pay ourselves—Great Britain will have to pay,

REPARATIONS AND WAR-DEBTS

France will have to pay and the rest of us. If Germany does not make the effort which we ask her to make, then the Allies must make it, and I think that we ought to give more attention to what Germany can actually pay.

Mr. Lloyd George: Certainly I have consideration for the Allies, and it is on account of this that we are trying to find a practical scheme for securing as much of this indemnity as we can, instead of confining ourselves to proposals which will only end in disillusionment, create false hopes, and prolong the agony of Europe without securing any substantial results. I think that I understand now what are M. Doumer's proposals. M. Doumer has pointed out that the nominal value of these goods has gone up, and that 10 milliards of gold marks before the war would mean a good deal more now in export. What M. Doumer has not pointed out, however, is that the same thing applies to imports, and that raw material which Germany has to import has also gone up in value, and that therefore the balance remains where it was— namely on the wrong side. However, as I understand M. Doumer's proposal it is this, that Germany should increase her exports to other countries, and diminish imports from other countries; that is, she should increase her exports to France and that she should diminish the imports she buys from France. Also the same thing should apply to Great Britain; that Great Britain should buy more goods from Germany, but that she should sell less to Germany. The same thing should apply to Belgium, and the same thing should also apply to Italy. Italy must sell fewer goods to Germany, but she must buy more from Germany. By that means we may get our 12 milliards of gold marks. I only want to understand what is M. Doumer's proposal in order to enable me to examine it with a better knowledge of the problem before me.

43

REPARATIONS AND WAR-DEBTS

M. Doumer: The Allies are not the only customers of Germany. *France and Great Britain will know how to defend their own industry.* The whole world, however, is open to Germany and one can rely on Germany that she will be able to find customers, and whilst limiting her expenses she will be able to find the necessary balance.

Mr. Lloyd George: How much of the 110 milliards has France assigned as material damage and how much as pensions?

M. Loucheur: Practically half.

M. Doumer: 54 milliards have been allocated for pensions and allowances and 57 milliards for actual damages.

Mr. Lloyd George: I would be glad if, in order to give further information, M. Doumer would have prepared an estimate of Germany's exports and imports with a balance that would enable the Allies to collect 12 milliards of gold marks. M. Doumer will quite understand that there is a vast difference between paying 30 milliards inside a country and paying 3 milliards outside. Each time we make a payment to America the sovereign depreciates in value and the same applies in the case of the franc. The Germans will experience exactly the same thing. I would like an estimate from M. Doumer of the sort of picture which he has in mind of this prosperous Germany with a tremendous excess of exports over imports which will enable the Allies to get these 12 milliards of gold marks.

M. Doumer undertook to produce a note embodying the required information.

On the following day I made on behalf of the British

Government a considered reply to M. Doumer's speech. It represented the deliberate policy of the British Government on this issue. I do not therefore apologize for quoting from it the following extracts:

"There can be no difference of opinion as far as the obligation of Germany is concerned. On the other hand, it is equally true that you can only exact damages and costs from the losing party to the extent of his capacity. These are the two principles upon which we are proceeding, and upon these two principles there is no difference of opinion. They are both acknowledged in the Treaty. The obligation of Germany, and also the fact that Germany cannot pay the whole of these damages and costs, is realized and acknowledged in the Treaty of Versailles.

"As far as the British Delegation is concerned, it is sometimes assumed that we are taking up a different attitude from that of France or other of our Allies. As a matter of fact, our position is identical. It is our interest that Germany should pay the highest figure that can be exacted from her. France gets 52 per cent of whatever is received from Germany by way of indemnity; Great Britain gets 22 per cent, and the higher the indemnity which is paid to France the higher the indemnity that will be received by Great Britain. Therefore, our interest is exactly the same as the interest of France, or of Belgium, or of Italy, that Germany should be made to pay the highest figure which can possibly be exacted. We have always acknowledged in Great Britain that France is first in the amount of suffering; her casualties have been greater; and she has suffered more in essentials than any other country—the losses of her youth. M. Doumer, with great eloquence, yesterday referred to a fact which France can never forget, and which the world will not forget, namely how generations of her young men have been cut down and the gaps which were apparent in every sphere of life in France. She had suffered more in the devastation of her country. I think I have seen the whole of those devastated areas. I spent Sunday after Sunday for months in visiting them from one end to another, and I realized, therefore, to the full what France has endured; how her country has been torn, and how it will take, not merely all the ingenuity and the resource and the courage of her great people to restore France, but how it will take years of time, even with all the ingenuity they can possibly display, to restore France to anything like the condition she was in before the war.

"Therefore, let it not be believed that, if we express any doubt about the figures which M. Doumer or anybody else puts forward as to the amount of the indemnity which can or ought to be exacted from Germany, that it is out of compassion for the people who have inflicted this great wrong so wantonly upon France—it is purely because we have doubts in our minds, after the most careful examination, not merely with our own experts, but with the experts of France, of Belgium, and of Italy, as to the possibility of exacting this sum.

"There is nothing worse than to devote your life to chasing exaggerated hopes. I have seen many individuals whose lives have been blighted by a process of that kind, and I should be sorry to see the Allied nations making that mistake—not satisfied with what they can reasonably hope to get, devoting their energies and their thought to pursuing something which is far beyond their reach. It is because I am anxious to redeem from such an error, not merely my own country, but the countries who are in close fraternity with ours—a fraternity which has been consecrated by much suffering on the part of all of us—that I am desirous that we should abandon high hopes which are beyond realization, and just devote ourselves to securing something which is reasonably within our reach.

REPARATIONS AND WAR-DEBTS

"If the Conference will bear with me I should like to say one additional word about the attitude of Great Britain and its financial position. M. Doumer, at the Conference yesterday, and M. Briand in the conversation which I have had since with him, emphasized the difficulty in making the Budget meet in France. I realized that, but it must not be imagined that there are no difficulties in Great Britain. France has suffered more in casualties and in damages, but as far as the cost of the war was concerned, the expenditure of Great Britain was heavier than that incurred by any belligerent. There were two or three reasons for that. We had to wage war outside our own country, and that is a much more expensive proceeding. We had to transport our own huge armies running into many millions, not merely to France, but to the East. We had, in addition to that, to equip and to maintain a gigantic navy. We had to add some thousands of craft to the navy we already had—to build and to adapt—and our navy cost us enormous sums of money. In addition, we had to do most of the sea-carrying for all the Allies. As a matter of fact, we carried more than half the American troops to France in 1918, although I never saw recognition of that fact in any statement by President Wilson except when he stated that, out of the millions carried to France, only a few hundred had been lost, and that in a British ship! All these facts have the effect of making the expenditure of Great Britain heavier than that of any other country. As a matter of fact, we had to spend upon the war £10,000,000,000 sterling —250 milliards of francs. It is true that our budget balances, but if our budget balances it is because, in order to do so, we imposed heavier taxation upon our people than any other country in the world has seen fit to impose upon its population up to the present. I put that in order to show that Great Britain has a deep financial interest in securing as high an indemnity as it possibly can.

47

REPARATIONS AND WAR-DEBTS

"Now what is the difficulty in exacting the total amount of our claims? It is a difficulty which is realized by all those who have been associated with the finances of these countries, more especially during the last few years. Before the war things went smoothly, and somehow or other we were able to get goods from abroad and to pay for them, and nobody asked any questions; nobody bothered much as to how it was done. But when the war forced us to increase enormously our purchases abroad, whilst at the same time we ceased to export abroad in order to pay for our purchases, we began to realize a fact which is a very fundamental one, although, even at the present moment, there are very few who seem to understand it, and I have seen men in very high positions upon whose intelligence it does not seem to have even dawned even to this hour, that there is a great difference between paying a debt inside your own country and paying it across the frontier.

"I have said that we spent over £10,000,000,000 sterling upon the war. As far as the expenditure in our own country was concerned, we were able to raise the money by one expedient or another, but when we came to purchase in America we found the most extraordinary difficulty in financing the transaction. We had to send gold. That, however, did not carry us very far. We had soon to sell most of the securities we had in North and South America, and in the end we had to borrow in America something like £1,000,000,000 sterling in order to be able to finance our purchases. . . . If America were to insist upon that payment I do not pretend that it would not place Great Britain in very considerable difficulties. If Germany had to pay the annuity of 12 milliards of marks asked by M. Doumer, within her own territory, she could do it, although not easily, but when you ask her to pay it outside her frontiers, not in paper marks, but in gold marks, that is, in marks which have full face value outside Germany, then it comes to difficulty. It is no use referring to the forests of Germany, and the railways of Germany, and the mines of Germany, and the land of Germany; you cannot transport the land of Germany or the forests of Germany over the frontier. Then take the railways of Germany; I shall have something to say about that later on, but supposing you seize the railways of Germany; you would have to collect your revenue in paper marks. Every man who travelled in a German railway train would pay his fare in paper marks. All the goods that are transported on the German railways would be paid for in paper marks, and at the end of it, if you took the whole revenue over to France, or to England, or to Belgium or to Italy, what good would it do you? Therefore, we have got to find out how much money Germany can pay outside her own frontier. M. Doumer said Germany can increase her exports and diminish her imports. Well, there is a limit to her diminution of imports. The vast majority of what she imports is either food or raw material, or essential machinery for her industries. If she does not get these her people will starve, or her industries will starve. Then she certainly could not pay an indemnity. If she increases her exports, where to? Her best customers, before the war, were Central Europe and Russia. It will take years before they can buy. Is Germany to increase her exports to England, or to France, or to Italy, or to Belgium? If she does she can only do so by displacing the labour of our own workmen. Is she to increase her exports to neutral markets? If she does she will do it at the expense of our own trade there.

"Now, these are questions for experts to consider. There is a margin which Germany can pay, but, as I ventured to say two years ago after the election in our own country, she must pay her indemnity in such a way as not to damage the industries of Allied countries, and it is a very difficult problem to find a means of exacting an indemnity in a way which will not injure the industries—the essential industries, the vital industries, of France, of Great Britain, of Italy, and of Belgium. That is a business which experts have been examining with great care. We have turned on some of the ablest experts which our respective countries could choose for this purpose. . . .

". . . If we discredit our experts and start afresh . . .

". . . We shall have another set of experts; and this will go on and on, and meanwhile Germany will go on printing paper marks, and not all the *camions* in France will be able to carry indemnity across the frontier because the mark will be so depreciated that it will require at least one *camion* for a gold franc! . . .

". . . Within limits, a speedy settlement is more important than the best settlement—within limits, of course. The failure to settle this question is helping to unsettle Europe. They tell me the same thing from America. The British Ambassador from America, whom I met last night, told me that America was convinced that the fact that there was no settlement of the indemnity question with Germany was having a very injurious effect upon trade, commerce and industry throughout the world. . . .

". . . As a matter of fact, you are not merely injuring your own country, but you are injuring your debtor, and a debtor is a person that you ought to cherish—you ought to look after him and you ought to see that he is in a condition to pay his debts. You certainly ought not to add to his difficulties, because if you do you will make him less capable of discharging his obligations to yourself. . . .

". . . I should like to hear some practical proposal. With respect to M. Doumer I do not think his proposal is even a debatable one. I have never heard any expert in his most sanguine moments, after giving time for the examination of

50

the problem, express an opinion that Germany was capable of paying 12 milliards of gold marks per annum—never. And I should like M. Doumer to name any expert, who has given time and thought to the problem, who would say so. I am not criticizing M. Doumer; he has only been in office for a few days. He has not had time to go into the question. He has not devoted as many hours to it as others have devoted weeks. I do not blame him for that. We have all approached the problem with the same sanguine hopes as inspired his speech. But when we came up against cold facts it left us more sober and considerably less hopeful in the matter of figures."

In the subsequent discussion, M. Jaspar, the Foreign Minister of Belgium, took part. He was evidently in a quandary. As an unequivocal supporter of France on all questions relating to the application of the Treaty, he was naturally anxious to support any thesis put forward by a French minister. On the other hand, Belgium is a country whose interests are predominantly industrial, and any artificial stimulus to German exports would undoubtedly damage its business. He pointed out that the Allies had to face a somewhat paradoxical situation. It was necessary for them to look after Germany's economic interests carefully and, at the same time, protect their own industries and demand reparation payments. M. Doumer's scheme to increase Germany's exports would undoubtedly imperil the industries of a country like Belgium, 40 per cent of the inhabitants of which were engaged in industry. Undoubtedly Germany could improve her budget position and in various ways she could substantially increase her revenue. The Allies must, however, be careful to secure themselves against a disastrous German competition with their own industries.

M. Doumer declared that he regretted to have to say that

my arguments had in no way shaken his belief in the scheme which he had been privileged to lay before the Conference on the previous occasion. After emphasizing the obligations imposed on Germany by the Treaty of Versailles and referring to the critical date May 1st, 1921, by which the claims of the Allies had to be submitted to Germany, he expressed the opinion that the Allies could settle the total indebtedness in time, and at all events whoever failed in this respect France would be sure of satisfying the requirement of the Treaty. He sincerely believed that Germany could pay the amount which he had indicated, and my criticism had not destroyed his belief in the least.

M. Briand, in his reply, made no endeavour to discuss Germany's capacity to pay. I have no recollection of his ever having at any of these conferences wandered into the jungle of statistics on any subject. He left this kind of adventure to M. Loucheur, who usually acted for him on these occasions. In this respect, he followed the example of M. Clemenceau, who had no appetite for figures. The robust commonsense of both these great men, however, led them to distrust sanguine estimates. On this occasion M. Briand's face was irradiated with a genial but cynical smile as he listened to M. Doumer rolling out his resounding forecast of the immense sums that could be expected from German forests. His reply gave no countenance to these estimates. He carefully shunned all reference to his Finance Minister's speech and said that difficulties of the kind which now confronted the Allies might be compared to a man confronted by a high wall who was forced to seek for some chink through which he might proceed. He felt confident that with goodwill the Allies would pass through the present difficulty. . . . "France was not unreasonable in this matter. French public opinion was always ready in the long run to bow before impossibilities but they must be real impossibilities, based on the complaints and grievances of the ex-enemy as realities. . . .

". . . French public opinion was intensely suspicious of the proceedings of Germany and demanded that the Allies should enquire the extent to which Germany was dissembling in this matter. For example, her budget was a most suspicious document. . . .

". . . France certainly would never agree to imperil her future by making what she would regard as a premature and unsatisfactory settlement at the present. . . .

". . . The French Government could not, therefore, stand by the Boulogne figure, but he personally was prepared to devote all his energies to reaching a satisfactory settlement on the basis he had suggested, and he would particularly accept the principle of the temporary annuities and investigate further the question of a lump sum. By adopting this policy the French people would gradually get informed as to the true position and perhaps learn the necessity for accepting a lower figure than they would contemplate at present."

I have quoted these discussions in considerable detail because they give an idea of the perplexities with which the Allies were confronted in enforcing the legal and moral obligation of the Central Powers to repair the damage caused by the war for which they were held responsible. They also reveal the differences that existed from the outset between France and Britain in their respective estimates of Germany's capacity.

CHAPTER VI

MAKING GERMANY PAY

An Allied conference which met at Spa on July 9th, 1920, settled the proportion in which any reparation payments forthcoming from Germany were to be divided between the victors. Subject to a special priority for Belgium to the extent of 2,000,000,000 gold marks, these proportions were: France, 52 per cent; Britain, 22 per cent; Italy, 10 per cent; Belgium, 8 per cent; and the other participants 8 per cent between them. In view of the benefit which Belgium actually secured, compared with her Allies, from her priority, these terms were later modified by the Paris Protocol of January, 1925, the Belgian share being reduced to $4\frac{1}{2}$ per cent, while the French was raised to 54.45 per cent and the British to 23.05 per cent.

I do not propose to trace out in detail all the tangled succession of conferences and negotiations between the Allies and Germany which arose out of the effort to secure a satisfactory measure of payment of reparations. As far as Germany is concerned, it is a painful tale of nervous and therefore clumsy struggles to adjust the demands of the Allies to her capacity for compliance with them. As far as the Allies are concerned, it is the story of a stubborn rearguard action fought against inexorable facts. On both sides governments had to fight battles on two fronts—the conference front and the home front.

The Treaty of Versailles had laid it down that pending the ascertainment by the Reparation Commission of the full bill

54

for damages, Germany should furnish by May 1st, 1921, the sum of 20,000,000,000 gold marks (£1,000,000,000) in cash or kind, out of which the cost of the Armies of Occupation and of foodstuffs and other supplies advanced to Germany should be paid, any balance being credited towards the reparation bill.

The Armies of Occupation were absorbing payments which ought to have gone to reparation account. With a disarmed Germany the occupation of her territory by foreign troops was a wanton and costly piece of provocation. For that reason I had resisted the proposal in 1919, but M. Clemenceau artfully persuaded President Wilson to agree to the French proposals. I then urged that the annual charge should be restricted. M. Loucheur agreed that the annual cost of the Armies of Occupation borne by Germany should not exceed £12,000,000 a year. By this agreement France did not abide. Actually the cost of these armies swallowed up more than the whole amount which the Reparation Commission had credited to Germany in respect of her payments up to May 1st, 1921. The French War Office were quartering a not inconsiderable part of their peace army on Germany—relieving their budget to that extent.

Long before May 1921 arrived, it became clear that neither the sum of 20 milliards nor (according to Allied computation) anything like it was being paid over. The French and Belgians were further greatly perturbed over difficulties that had arisen in the carrying through of Germany's disarmament. A conference was held in London in March 1921, at which the attitude of the German representatives appeared so unsatisfactory, more particularly on the subject of disarmament, that it was decided to bring further pressure to bear by extending the area of occupied territory to take in the Rhineland industrial towns of Düsseldorf, Duisberg and Ruhrort.

55

That Germany had at that time failed to fulfil entirely the disarmament obligations laid on her by the Treaty of Versailles can hardly be questioned. The Government of the Reich was doing its best, but it was not strong enough to coerce some of the recalcitrant elements of Germany into submission. Even some weeks later, at the London Conference of April 30th, M. Briand had to report that Germany was still refusing compliance with the conditions laid down by the Military Commission on Disarmament, and that in respect of Bavaria a formal statement had been published that disarmament should not take place. "The president of the Bavarian Council had stated that there were 300,000 rifles and machine guns, and a reserve of 1,000 cannon, quite ready for use," said M. Briand. "These weapons France regarded as aimed at her heart." Germany had failed to make the deliveries of armaments to which she had agreed at Spa. She had not suppressed the Einwohnerwehren and the Sicherheitspolizei, nor carried out her undertakings in respect of aërial material, aircraft manufacture and the reduction of shell-making factories. In fact, he declared, she was declining to carry out her obligations.

France was angry over this breach of faith. I wish some of this moral indignation would now operate against her own statesmen who decline to carry out that part of the Treaty which imposed a solemn obligation on France to follow the example Germany had been forced to set in respect of disarmament. Germany failed at the end of nineteen months to complete her full programme of disarmament. A French army occupied her towns and bullied her at the point of the bayonet into compliance. Eleven years have elapsed since then, and French ministers are still arguing at Geneva whether they should carry out one-tenth of their treaty obligations in respect of disarmament.

More dubious is the issue whether Germany was to any

serious extent deliberately defaulting over payment of reparations. The British Government had publicly recognized two years before that the transfer of large sums across her frontiers by a war-exhausted country would be a very difficult operation, and later history has proved how severe are the limits which economic laws impose upon such a transaction. But throughout the negotiations of those years, successive French ministers showed a most extraordinary stubbornness —not to say obtuseness—in this respect. They acted as though they thought that economic laws could be changed or reversed, like an Act of Parliament, by a vote of the majority, or suspended in their operation by military force. If a payment that had been ordained was not fully made, they refused to believe that the hard facts of the economic situation might be responsible. In their view the only possible cause was deliberate fraud and default by Germany.

The fullest excuse must be admitted for them when we remember what the French and Belgian nations had just suffered at German hands. Their judgment was clouded by the smart of suffering from horrible wounds still unhealed, as well as by feelings of fear rooted in memories of horror. But to admit that their attitude was excusable is not to say that it was justified. The distrust and ruthlessness that swayed their judgment at all the conferences on reparations, that later led them to the costly stupidity of the Ruhr invasion, and even as recently as last year caused them to palter over-long with the Hoover moratorium proposal, are to a very high degree responsible for the continued unsettlement of Europe and the world-wide economic depression which has now supervened.

A good illustration of the French attitude to the reparation issue was supplied by the proposal of that most reasonable and sagacious of French ministers, M. Briand, to which I refer a little further on, that as a preliminary to formulating our demands on Germany for payment of the sum fixed by the Reparation Commission as her total liability we should forthwith occupy the Ruhr, for the sake of the moral effect which the dislocation of that vital industrial area would produce upon the German commercial magnates. But M. Briand was amenable to the appeals of reason, and in the course of prolonged discussions he modified his original demand. On the other hand, arguments reinforced by irrefutable facts and figures were as fruitless with M. Poincaré as a shower on the Sahara.

The occupation of the Rhineland towns, applied as a military sanction to render the German Government more pliable, may have eased the task of the Allied representatives supervising disarmament. But it did not improve Germany's economic condition, upon which the payment of reparations ultimately depended: quite the reverse. France professed childlike faith in the efficacy of such military sanctions as a means of extracting money from Germany, and wished to press forward with the occupation of town after town—as King John is said to have pulled out the teeth of Jews—until the cash was forthcoming. But the British Government determined to oppose such profitless bullying, and while I was in office, no further extension of the occupied area was made.

Amid this uneasy atmosphere, the Reparation Commission reported, on April 27th, 1921, its findings as to the total bill for damages chargeable against Germany in accordance with the Reparation Clauses of the Versailles Treaty. This amounted, as already stated, to 132,000,000,000 gold marks —say £6,600,000,000.

As to the justice of this figure, I may say that at the first session of the Allied Conference which met three days later in London, to consider the terms of payment to be imposed upon Germany, I asked Sir John Bradbury, the British representative on the Reparation Commission, in the presence of the leading statesmen of France, Belgium, Italy and Japan, whether the Commission held this to be a fair and moderate amount, neither extravagant nor exaggerated, having regard to the damage sustained; prefacing my question with the statement that he need not answer it unless he cared to do so. He replied that of course he could not speak for the Reparation Commission as a whole, but his own personal view was that the sum fixed was not an excessive one, and was similar in character to that which would have been fixed by an impartial British jury in a claim against a railway company; that was to say, it represented not a strictly scientific assessment of damage, but an approximate and at the same time an equitable settlement. It is fair to the Reparation Commission to point out that their assessment of the damage was made at a time when prices were exceptionally high. The actual cost of repairs turned out to be considerably below the estimate. The figure for pensions was calculated actuarily and is unchallengeable.

It was exceedingly hard at this conference to induce the representatives of France and Belgium, urged on as they were by a public opinion behind them which was still excited and unrelenting, to adopt a reasonably judicial attitude to the matters under discussion. When Sir John Bradbury announced the figure that the Reparation Commission had fixed, M. Briand declared that M. Tardieu would be certain to attack him as regards the amount fixed, and would press him to state why he had not insisted on a higher figure! M. Tardieu had been since the war coming into prominence as the champion of all the extremist demands of France—the annexation of the left bank of the Rhine and a crushing indemnity. I had to point out that "it would be a serious matter if the Allied Governments, or any of them, had put pressure upon the Reparation Commission to fix a higher

59

figure than the Commission thought equitable." M. Briand accepted this view of the judicial position of the Commission.

The French and Belgians were insistent that we should proceed at once, before even proposing to the Germans any terms for settlement of their debt, to occupy the Ruhr and hold its industries and coalfields as a security for payment. The aim of this proposed action was punitive and destructive rather than economic. They had formed no idea as to how long the occupation should continue, or on what conditions it should be terminated. M. Briand claimed that the French Government did not intend to dismember Germany, and would withdraw their troops as soon as guarantees had been given by the German Government that Germany would discharge her obligations. But when I pressed him to say what was the sort of guarantee which the French would require before the French troops were withdrawn, he replied that it was impossible for him to say what guarantees would be satisfactory. He was only clear that no promises or undertakings on the part of Germany would be satisfactory— they would be mere scraps of paper, which might be dishonoured. I have never seen M. Briand so unreasonable and implacable. It was quite contrary to his wont. I can only explain it by recalling the fact that there was at that time a wave of impatience and resentment passing over Parisian opinion at the concessions which had been then recently made by M. Briand's predecessor in respect of the payment of reparations by Germany and at the delay and reluctance on the latter's part to surrender her military equipment in accordance with the terms of the Treaty.

When I pointed out that in my view the immediate occupation of the Ruhr, before Germany had been given a chance to accept or refuse the terms of payment prepared by the Reparation Commission, would be legally without justification under the Versailles Treaty, would be morally wrong and economically a blunder, and that the British Government could not consent to it, M. Briand pleaded with me to make some concession, as he declared that if he went back to Paris without having arranged to occupy the Ruhr, his government would fall forthwith and be replaced by one under M. Poincaré—who would defy the rest of the Allies and the public opinion of the world and take his own steps with Germany.

With the utmost difficulty I succeeded in persuading M. Briand and M. Jaspar (the Belgian Foreign Minister, whose sympathy with France was even more intransigent) after discussions lasting several days, to abandon their project for an immediate invasion of the Ruhr, and to consent to adhere to the terms of the Treaty by first placing before Germany the proposals of the Reparation Commission for methods of payment; occupation of the Ruhr to take place only if Germany herself broke the Treaty by flatly refusing to accept the repayment terms laid down by the Commission. In the event, Germany wisely accepted the terms, and the danger of immediate military sanctions was averted.

The terms in question were actually a good deal more lenient, as well as more practicable, than a blank insistence on repayment within thirty years—the period appointed in the Treaty—of principal and interest on the full sum of 132,000,000,000 marks. Originating with the British financial experts, and ultimately adopted by the Commission, they were an attempt to adjust the bill to Germany's capacity to pay.

The total of 132,000,000,000, less any balance available for reparation account from sums already paid, but increased by the Belgian war debt, which Germany had undertaken to settle, was split up into three parts, to be paid for by the issue of three series of bonds.

Series "A" were to be bonds for 12,000,000,000 gold

marks, to be prepared and issued by July 1st, 1921, on which Germany was to pay 6 per cent per annum, being 5 per cent interest, and 1 per cent sinking fund, towards amortization of the bonds.

Series "B" were to be bonds for 38,000,000,000 gold marks, created and delivered by November 1st, 1921, with the same arrangements as to rate of interest and sinking fund.

These two series represented a capital payment of 50,000,000,000 gold marks—say £2,500,000,000. That was the sum suggested by the German negotiators at Versailles.

The remainder of the reparation debt—80,000,000,000 marks—was left over with the stipulation that if and when Germany was able to make any greater annual payments than those required for service of the "A" and "B" bonds, the Reparation Commission should issue "C" bonds for as much of this sum as German finance could bear. Germany had to deposit these "C" bonds with the Commission by November 1st in readiness for such issues; and if issued, they would carry from date of issue the same conditions as to interest and sinking fund. But it was recognized that there was no near prospect of their having any value at all and for all practical purposes the London Conference cancelled over a million marks of the total indemnity, and no one after this date ever attempted to resume this portion of the claim except for one tentative suggestion by M. Poincaré that the "C" bonds should be utilized to settle the outstanding claims of America and Britain in respect of war debts—a proposal not pressed seriously even by him.

Germany was required to pay 2,000,000,000 gold marks a year towards service of these bonds, together with 26 per cent of the value of her exports. These two items together were estimated to come to about 3,000,000,000 gold marks, or the requisite 6 per cent for the service of the 50,000,000,000 in bonds "A" and "B." In practical effect, therefore, this demand was no larger than the offer which Germany had herself made via the U.S.A. on April 24th, to pay off a capital sum of 50,000,000,000 by annuities totalling over 200,000,000,000 over a term of years. By implication, although not specifically, it was acknowledged that payment by Germany of principal and interest on more than 50,000,000,000 gold marks was impracticable.

This was a considerable concession. Yet it proved insufficient to bring down the demand on Germany to a point within her capacity to pay. As time went on, she was found to be internally and externally bankrupt. Whether the internal bankruptcy was wholly unavoidable in view of her exhaustion after a prolonged war, and the resources in cash, kind and territory which had already been alienated under the peace settlement, or whether it was contributed to by the action of her big business magnates, may be open to discussion. In view of the partial bankruptcy which also overtook France, Belgium and Italy, as expressed in the permanent devaluation of their currency, it is likely that in any case Germany could not have avoided her disaster. But the effort to pay across her frontier a sum exceeding what her export trade made possible hastened her collapse.

Germany was required under the settlement to pay a first instalment of 1,000,000,000 gold marks by the end of August 1921. To do this, she had to secure foreign currency for this amount. The moment she attempted to buy such foreign currency, the mark—already much depreciated—began to tumble again. At once, private citizens in Germany set about turning their own holdings of marks into foreign currency, and swept the market bare. The mark, ordinarily worth a shilling, had in June 1921 been fifteen to the shilling, but by September it had fallen to twenty-five to the shilling. By November it was seventy-five to the shilling. Yields of internal taxation failed to rise at a rate even remotely

63

approaching this speedy decline in external value. The tax-gatherer never could catch up with the flying mark. It became clear that in 1922 the German Government would not be able to maintain its due payments. The internal value of the mark was also falling, so that by the time taxes reached the treasury they were worth far less than when they were assessed, and were inadequate for the rising costs of the government. So the budget showed only a deficit, out of which to pay reparations.

The country laboured under the difficulty that its Republican government was new and as yet somewhat insecure, and that the method adopted of organizing industry in Germany during the war for the purpose of munition production had resulted in the formation of immensely powerful trusts and combines in private hands, which would brook no dictation. The government found itself unable to obtain control even of such moderate foreign credits as these industries developed, for the purpose of financing a loan with which to pay its reparation instalments; and its own credit was worthless for the purpose.

In view of these difficulties it was unfortunate that nothing had been done to attempt a practical application of the proposal put forward by the Germans at the time the Treaty of Versailles was being drawn up, whereby they should themselves carry out reconstruction work in the devastated area. Various attempts had been made by them to open negotiations for doing this work in whole or in part; but France always raised objections on one ground or another. The fact was, of course, that the French contractors who undertook the work of reconstruction had not the slightest intention of letting the job pass into German hands; and it would also have been very difficult for any government in France to concur in the importation of German workmen so long as any Frenchmen were out of work. When pressing the acceptance of the German offer on French ministers we were assured that the French trade unions were inexorably hostile to any such schemes. At the same time, there can be little question that if France was really in desperate need of help to carry out this reconstruction work, the most certain way of obtaining it would have been to let Germany perform the task. And it becomes less easy to reproach Germany for failing to make good the damage she wrought, when she can truly retort that she offered to do so, but was not permitted.

By the end of 1921 it was clear that the sums due in January and February 1922 would not be forthcoming, and on December 14th, 1921, Germany applied for a moratorium. Dr. Rathenau also came to see me in London, to solicit the sympathetic attitude of this country to some measure of alleviation of the pressure on Germany. I was of the opinion that he made out his case; but the Reparation Commission, which considered the German demand on December 29th, could not come to an agreement on the issue. This is one of the occasions when the absence of an American delegate on the Commission proved fatal to wise action.

With M. Briand's consent I therefore invited the German Government to send a delegation to discuss the matter with the Allied Governments who were to meet soon at Cannes. For a time there was at this conference a real hope that Germany might secure both an immediate moratorium for the next sums due, and a reduction in the total amount she would be required to pay during the year. The suggestion I had discussed with Herr Rathenau was a limitation of cash payments for 1922 to 500,000,000 gold marks, with a continuance of the reparation payments in kind. At Cannes, the limitation of gold payments to not more than 720,000,000 marks seemed possible of general acceptance.

The Cannes conference was remarkable for the able,

impressive and tenacious fight put up by Herr Rathenau to save his country from being driven into insolvency by exactions beyond her capacity to bear. A few months later he was shot down like a wolf in the streets of Berlin by one of his own fellow countrymen. Unhappily, in the middle of a powerful speech from Herr Rathenau, news came that M. Briand's ministry in France had fallen, through distrust of the concessions he was rumoured to be making to the Germans. He was superseded by M. Poincaré, whose opinions on everything German—as we shall see later—were those of a Salvation Army captain about the devil. All concessions to that evil and dangerous personage were not only a mistake but a sin. Inevitably the Cannes conference broke up without result. M. Poincaré had no use for it. He knew how to get money out of Germany—by the lash!

To understand what ensued on the deposition of M. Briand and the accession of M. Poincaré to office we must realize the essential difference in the outlook of these statesmen. M. Briand was a Breton born and bred on a coast never successfully raided for centuries by a foreign invader. M. Poincaré was a Lorrainer born in a province repeatedly overrun and ravaged by Teutonic hosts—twice within living memory and several times within the last 150 years. He himself twice witnessed the occupation of his own cherished home by German troops. He remembers, and saw with his own eyes, the agony of tearing from the side of France a part of the beloved province to which he belonged. His village was left in France, but for all the impressionable years of his boyhood he was within sight of the German posts planted in the sacred soil of *la patrie*. Many a time during his boyish wanderings he must have seen the hated *pickelhaube* patrolling the ransacked lands of Lorraine. Apart from upbringing there were essential differences of temperamental and intellectual quality between the two statesmen. M. Briand

66

is genial, humorous, tolerant, broadminded and warm-hearted. He has the imagination and suppleness of mind of a purely Celtic race. He is essentially an appeaser. M. Poincaré is cold, reserved, rigid, with a mind of unimaginative and ungovernable legalism. He has neither humour nor good humour. In conference he was dour and morose. In appearance he is obviously Flemish by race. He is the most un-French Frenchman I ever met. His judgment on anything affecting the treatment of Germany was further upset by an undignified experience to which he was driven at the beginning of the war by the relentless Teuton. In the dead of night he fled from his presidential palace to an obscure wayside station in order to catch an express for Bordeaux which would enable him to put hundreds of miles between him and the abhorred helmets from across the Rhine.

It is related of M. Clemenceau that when he was asked, as the Germans had reached a point within a few leagues of Paris, whether he did not think the Government and Parliament ought to leave at once, he replied, "Yes, I agree; I think we are too far from the front."

M. Poincaré never forgot the humiliation of his flight. The fact that the Germans never got into Paris made the hegira look silly and pusillanimous. The episode intensified an enmity towards the Germans which was already well in his marrow. He never concealed his dislike for the Treaty of Versailles. For him a treaty of peace with prostrate Germany was a supreme opportunity for reducing this age-long foe of his country to utter impotence. He was not concerned about a just, and least of all, a magnanimous peace. He wanted to cripple Germany, and render her impotent for future aggression. Clemenceau had, in his view, thrown away for ever a great chance for achieving French security if not supremacy in the secular struggle between Gaul and Teuton. But now that the Treaty had been signed, all that could be done to attain his aim was to administer the penal clauses with relentless legality. When German questions had to be dealt with such a man could not be expected to be normal. Scrupulously fair and straight in all his dealings in the ordinary affairs of life, he was neither where Germany was concerned. The fall of M. Briand sent the world rolling towards the catastrophe which culminated in 1931. Had he remained in office, European appeasement from the Urals to the Rhine might have been reached in 1922 and the troubles of the last ten years which fermented into disaster in 1931 would have been averted.

The strength of M. Poincaré's undoubted hold on a large section of opinion lies in the general fear of Germany which is rooted more particularly in the populous towns and provinces, adjacent to the German frontier. This extends as far as the capital. When one recalls the lessons of 1814, 1870 and 1914–18 it is not to be wondered at that those who dwell within daily sight of the scars due to the tearing wounds inflicted by Teutonic hands on their living land should have a natural apprehension lest the same calamities should befall again. Stripped of some of its richest provinces, Germany has still a population 50 per cent above that of France. The German is industrious, intelligent and resourceful, and although he is poor to-day such qualities soon make riches. He will therefore, so Frenchmen realize, once more become a formidable menace. The Teuton is on the French nerves. This accounts for the anxiety to keep him chained by treaties, impoverished by levies, and overawed by armaments.

When M. Briand disappeared from Cannes the Reparation Commission had to step in and grant Germany a temporary moratorium on condition of payment by her every ten years of 31,000,000 gold marks—representing the value of the 25 per cent levy on exports and the customs duties pledged for reparations. On March 21st it followed this up by offering a moratorium for 1922, whereby Germany's payments for the year would be limited to 720,000,000 gold marks in cash, and deliveries in kind to the value of 1,450,000,000 gold marks, but subject to Germany imposing on itself additional taxation to a specified amount, and admitting a far-reaching control of its finances by the Commission's Committee of Guarantees. These last conditions were rejected by Germany, and the moratorium was subsequently granted without them.

On the day when the German reply was handed to the Commission at Paris, the International Conference of Genoa met for its first session. It had been arranged for at Cannes, delegates being invited from all European states, including Russia, to discuss the economic and financial reconstruction of Central and Eastern Europe. War debts and reparations were, of course, a vital factor in any such discussion, but M. Poincaré had made it an absolute condition for the participation of France that reparations should not be dealt with—thus dooming the gathering to partial impotence. He would not himself come near Genoa, but it is recorded that during the sitting of the conference he kept up a long-range bombardment against the conference, and that he sent to M. Barthou no fewer than a thousand telegraphic messages whose sole purpose was to thwart all efforts at European appeasement. While the conference was sitting he made a speech at Bar-le-Duc in which he reasserted that France would only remain at Genoa on condition that no concessions were made to Germany, and threatened that if Germany failed to meet her reparation instalment at the end of May, France would invade the Ruhr, with or without the agreement and co-operation of her Allies.

This hankering on the part of French governments for an invasion of the Ruhr I had already to combat a year previously at the London conference. So long as I remained in office, I was able to postpone the carrying out of the threat. But it was a fixed idea with the extremer element in France, of which M. Poincaré was the prophet. Ostensibly the purpose was to "bring Germany to her senses," and compel her to pay up—though how the temporary severance of her chief industrial region was to make it easier for her to pay could never be explained. The true motive with the Rhine party in France was to bring Germany to the ground, with possibly a secret hope of detaching this rich district from the Reich as a separate republic, and linking it afterwards in some way with French industry. There was a powerful body of opinion in Paris which was firmly convinced that a Rhineland confederation friendly to France and in alliance with France could be resurrected. It had happened in the nineteenth century; why not in the twentieth? M. Clemenceau resolutely discouraged every attempt to foster intrigues to work up separatist movements inside Germany. But during the French occupation of the Ruhr many sporadic efforts were made to set up such an independent state in the Rhineland. They were not repressed or discouraged by the French authorities, and of course German forces could not operate in the invaded area to suppress these fissiparous designs. In spite of everything, they ignominiously failed. German patriotism was unbreakable.

The truth is, that any practical, common-sense examination of the reparation problem was ruled out of court when M. Poincaré was in charge of the French case. In August 1922 he came to represent his country in London at an Allied conference, invited by me when Germany had applied for a complete moratorium until the end of 1924, and it had become evident that she was at present incapable of making even the modified payments required under the partial moratorium she had been granted. His proposals at this conference showed either a total inability to grasp even the

alphabet of economic conditions governing payments from
one country to another, or a sinister resolve to engineer a
German default under the Treaty which would justify an
invasion of the Westphalian minefields with ulterior possibilities of detaching them from the German Fatherland.

Declaring that he wished to place all his cards on the table,
M. Poincaré at this conference urged that the Allies should
take over the German customs; that they should expropriate
the State mines and State forests; require the surrender to
them of the majority of the shares in a number of prosperous
German factories; and even proceed to collect the taxes in
the occupied provinces. He further insisted that this ruthless
dragooning of Germany should be carried through without
even waiting for a verdict from the Reparation Commission
that Germany was in deliberate default—the sole condition
on account of which any such additional sanctions could
under the Treaty be imposed.

From this programme I dissented most strongly. I pointed
out that M. Poincaré's proposal meant smashing the Treaty
and writing a new one. He had given a most extraordinary
reason for his proposal. The Germans had asked for a moratorium. They had a perfect right under the Treaty to do so
on the plea of incapacity to pay. The Allies were being asked
by M. Poincaré to reply that the mere fact that the Germans
had asked for a moratorium justified the Allies in altering
the Treaty. The Reparation Commission, I pointed out, was
not a German invention or for their convenience, but an
instrument forced on Germany by the Allies. It contained no
impartial persons at all, and no representative of the debtor
countries, for all its members were furnished by the creditor
countries. "M. Poincaré says that he cannot trust the Reparation Commission to do what he wants, so he would
brush it aside, and act without Germany having been declared
in default. He wishes to go straight into Germany and get

his own reparations. If he likes to break the Treaty, he must do it alone. I stand by the Treaty."

Poincaré suggested that each of the Allied Governments should instruct its own commissioner on the Reparation Commission to declare Germany in wilful default, so that sanctions could be lawfully applied under the Treaty, but I insisted that as the Commission was a judicial body on this issue, any such direction would be unjustifiable.

M. Poincaré professed a simple belief that the marks collected on reparation accounts could be cashed at their exchange value at that date. He did not realize that there would be no buyer and that the moment you placed a large consignment on the market the mark would crash to un-pickable atoms. As to M. Poincaré's proposals for the seizure of the forests and mines; the extension of the custom service; levying of taxation: I urged that nothing would be forth-coming from them but *paper marks*. Already 1,500,000,000 of paper marks had been collected by the German customs on Allied reparation account, which the Reparation Commis-sion dare not cash, because they would get hardly anything for them, and if they attempted to realize, the mark exchange would depreciate still further. Yet the holding of such large sums of paper marks made the recovery of the exchange very problematical. The management of the forests and mines by the Allies would depend almost entirely for its success on the goodwill of the German workman, who could easily convert a profitable undertaking into a bankrupt one—for, I pointed out, the employment of forced labour was of course unthink-able. One was in fact brought up against the old proposi-tion, viz., how to transmit across the border these natural resources, which was the whole crux of reparations.*

*There is no more effective exposure of the proposal for seizing German mines, State forests, railways and customs than that given by M. Tardieu in his *Truth about the Treaty*, page 334:—

"Control public utilities? That is easy to say. But who can fail to see that

REPARATIONS AND WAR-DEBTS

The Italian representative, Signor Schanzer, a distinguished banker, expressed himself in substantial agreement with my view, and M. Theunis, the Belgian Prime Minister, an eminently sane and intelligent statesman with a thorough knowledge of finance, sounded a warning note as to the possible after-effects of M. Poincaré's policy.

This conference continued for a week, and finally broke up without coming to a decision. It proved impossible to convince M. Poincaré of the futility of amassing vast quantities of German paper marks by means of measures which would destroy the industrial and financial organization of Germany and finally ensure that those marks should be permanently valueless. He was obstinately sure that the exploitation of German forests could easily be carried out under the supervision of the Allied military authorities, and that it would be practicable for them to control the Reichsbank and force up the value of the mark. Above all, he insisted that whether Germany could or could not pay during the next few months, no moratorium should be granted to her without the application of what he called "guarantees"— in other words, occupation of the Ruhr and the other drastic measures he had proposed. By the end of the conference he stood alone in this attitude. Even the Belgian representatives,

---

in order to do it an enormous personnel would have been necessary. Under the circumstances control would have meant operation, otherwise control would have been a sham. Who can fail to see that such a method adopted because of the debtor's refusal to pay, that is to say with the ever-present possibility of conflict, would have entailed in addition to the collecting and operating personnel, a personnel of protection—which means an armed force—thus leading inevitably to that total and prolonged occupation of German territory that none of the Allies would consent to and which was out of the question because the necessary forces were not available. To hold the ports, the customs, the railways, the mines, meant supplying customs officials, station masters, engineers, etc., and called for military police everywhere. No one would have risked such an adventure without the prospect of real advantage. But what advantage would there have been? That is precisely what the peace-makers inquired into, and what those who heap retrospective criticism upon them seem to ignore."

closely though they stood by France as a rule, refused to support such folly as this, and I warned M. Poincaré as plainly as I could that if he proceeded with independent action on the lines he threatened, he might ultimately destroy the Treaty of Versailles and the Entente. If he thought that worth doing for the sake of a few tons of paper marks, it was for him to decide.

The conference having decided nothing, the Reparation Commission was quite properly left to deal with the situation, and effected a compromise by accepting German bills, guaranteed by the Reichsbank, in lieu of further cash payments for 1922. Nothing was settled, however, as to the grant of a further moratorium for 1923 and 1924. Throughout the autumn of 1922, M. Poincaré Sunday after Sunday visited different French towns, to chant his weekly "hymn of hate" against Germany, and to breathe out threats of drastic action. Plan after plan was laid before the Reparation Commission by the British, Italian or Belgian delegates, all to be vetoed by the French delegate under instructions from M. Poincaré. In October 1922 my own seventeen years' spell of office came to an end, and Mr. Bonar Law replaced me as Prime Minister, but while this involved no departure from the fundamental attitude of this country to the reparation problem, it also brought about no improvement in Franco-British relations on the issue.

It is hard to understand M. Poincaré's conduct at that time except on the assumption that he was dominated by the fixed idea of carrying out the Ruhr invasion and dealing a smashing and rending blow not only at German industry but at German unity. He could not have seriously supposed, having regard to the facts which were available to him about Germany's financial condition, that his programme would really succeed in extracting full payment from a country in such a plight. Had his real object been to get cash from Germany, there was

74

the unanimous verdict of all the highest experts confronting him, that a temporary moratorium and no interference with Germany's industries were essential conditions. But he rejected every plan put forward, insulted Mr. J. P. Morgan and the group of big international bankers who were seeking to plan a sound basis for a loan to restore German finances, and after having wrecked Allied unity, held all Europe in suspense and chaos for the rest of the year, while the German mark fell till it was 160 to the penny. Ultimately it reduced the French franc to one-fifth of its pre-war value.

On January 2nd, 1923, an Allied conference met in Paris. The British conference was headed by Mr. Bonar Law, who protested vigorously against the Poincaré proposals. As a result the conference broke up in less than two days, after M. Poincaré had made it clear that he would accept no plan but his own—a plan that would have granted only a slight reduction in Germany's immediate payments, while incorporating all the coercive measures he had propounded in August. Mr. Bonar Law had left the conference in disgust before its conclusion.

Upon this breakdown, M. Poincaré demanded of the Reparation Commission a verdict that Germany was in voluntary default in her coal deliveries—a verdict duly delivered by a majority of the Commission on January 9th, the British representative dissenting; and on January 11th the French proceeded to invade the Ruhr—an act of military aggression against a disarmed nation that was as unjustified as it was to prove unprofitable.

The invasion of the Ruhr by the French and their Belgian Allies naturally brought to an end for the time being all voluntary payment of reparations by Germany. She treated the invasion as an act of war, to which in her disarmed state she could offer only passive resistance. The inhabitants of the occupied district under the circumstances behaved with great

75

restraint. There was no disorder, though the workers downed tools, and the cost of their maintenance fell on the Reich, and finally helped to wreck the mark and bankrupt the government. In 1924 the Dawes Committee, which was appointed by the Reparation Commission at the end of 1923, furnished a scheme for a new schedule of reparation payments, conditional upon the abandonment of the Ruhr occupation and the restoration of Germany to her sovereignty over her territory, and the fall of the Poincaré ministry in France made it possible for the Allies to come to agreement on these terms. A conference met in London on July 16th, 1924, at which the Dawes Plan was accepted, and conditions for its working laid down. These included provisions which would make it impossible in the future for M. Poincaré to hurl Europe into chaos by using reparations as a pretext for attacks upon Germany's territory and industrial life.

Therewith closed the dismal and tragic episode of the Ruhr occupation, which had caused untold misery to the many millions of Central Europe, had put back the clock of post-war reconstruction throughout the world, intensified unemployment problems and industrial depression, and had signally failed in its main object of extracting reparations from Germany. Although the French and Belgians had imposed drastic levies on the rich industrial district they occupied, sequestered the taxes in the area and exacted fines and requisitions from the inhabitants, over a period of nearly 20 months, the total net proceeds they claim to have secured in cash and kind during this period (January 11th, 1923 to September 1st, 1924) amounted to under £40,000,000. From this the expenses of the occupation had to be deducted.

They would have received more in cash and in kind had they not occupied the Ruhr, and would have profited more on balance. France and Belgium lost by this ill-conditioned and headlong adventure. The greatest loss of all was the

76

alienation of Allied and world sympathy and goodwill. I need not examine in detail here the terms of the Dawes Plan. It is enough to say that it assessed the amount Germany should be required to pay in a normal year as 2,500,000,000 gold marks—with a possible increase after 1930 if the index of prosperity for Germany warranted it. This may be compared with the terms laid down in 1921 by the Reparation Commission of 2,000,000,000 gold marks a year, plus a 26 per cent levy on exports, estimated to yield about another 1,000,000,000. The Dawes Plan therefore assessed Germany's capacity to pay 500,000,000 gold marks a year less than the Reparation Commission had done in 1921.

CHAPTER VII

THE PROBLEM OF EXTERNAL PAYMENT

THE events narrated in the foregoing chapters show clearly enough how difficult a task it was for the Allied statesmen to estimate in advance what sums could be extracted from Germany, and how wise was the decision reached at Versailles not to lay down in the Treaty a fixed sum which would certainly have proved to be far beyond her capacity to pay.

In dealing with this question of reparations, we were handicapped by the fact that hardly any previous experience was available to guide us in judging the extent to which it would be possible to transfer huge sums of money across the frontier from Germany to other States. The only previous example of a comparable nature was that of the indemnity of £200,000,000 which France was required to pay to Germany after the Franco-Prussian War. This was an insignificant sum beside the amount it was desired to levy on Germany, and a considerable portion of it had been transferred in the form of gold. Even at that, France had found it necessary to borrow extensively from other nations in order to secure the funds wherewith to discharge her debt. The extensive liabilities incurred by the Southern States of the U.S.A. to British investors for war loans during the American Civil War have never been paid at all.

But it was obvious that the total amount which Germany would be required to pay in reparations must be vastly greater than her available gold supply. We have seen that the total fixed by the Reparation Commission was £6,600,000,000.

78

REPARATIONS AND WAR-DEBTS

But in 1918-19 the total world stock of monetary gold (including the gold reserves of every country) was only £1,900,000,000. When the Armistice was signed, Germany held stocks of gold to the value of £115,000,000; but by September 1919 this had been reduced to £55,000,000 through expenditure on food, on raw materials for home industries, and on settlement of debts due to neutrals. If reparations were to be paid, they must be paid in merchandise.

Such exports would be on a very different footing from the movements of goods which normally take place in commercial transactions with a new and developing country, where food and raw materials are being produced in ever-increasing quantities and are exported in payment for loans, furnished by manufacturing countries to the borrowing State in the form of machinery, railway equipment, and the materials for large constructive works to promote its development. Britain has traditionally employed its favourable balance of trade to grant loans of this character to new countries such as Australia and the Argentine—and indeed did so formerly to the United States; and the annual payments these countries were required to make in interest and liquidation of these debts have in practice been possible for two reasons: first, that their productive capacity had been greatly stimulated and entirely made profitable by the developments which such loans promoted; and second, that the food and raw materials which were their principal products were urgently required by us to supplement our inadequate internal supplies for our large industrial population.

It is obvious that the payment of reparations presented a very different problem. It was to be a payment from one fully developed manufacturing country to other countries similarly developed, and must therefore largely consist of merchandise which these countries would normally produce themselves; and it was made in respect of a liability which did not arise

79

from the receipt of stimulating loans to foster the capacity of the debtor country to pay. On the contrary, Germany was exhausted by the very effort which created her liability.

These same difficulties, it may be noted in passing, arose also in connection with the payment of inter-Allied debts.

A sharp distinction must be drawn between the problem of reparations and war-debts which have to be settled across the frontier and those which are internal. A country's internal debt is owed by the government to its own nationals and is settled by the simple process of taking from all nationals in taxation what is paid out to a large number of them in dividend and amortization. I will not here enter on a discussion of the debatable question of the precise extent to which these internal liabilities involve a definite loss to the country which incurs them, either in respect of the unproductive waste of material and human effort in which the sums they represent were expended, or through their fostering fresh expansions of the rentier class, on a scale which may make it injuriously parasitic upon the workers. It will suffice to point out that they do not necessarily affect a country's financial status *vis-à-vis* other nations, although they involve a certain measure of redistribution of purchasing power between its own citizens. But the payment of debts or reparations across the frontier implies a definite impoverishment of the nation to the full extent of the amount handed over. Experience has also shown that grave embarrassment is suffered by the trade of the creditor country which is required to receive either manufactures which it would normally produce itself, or gold, which must lie heaped up unproductively in its strong rooms with disastrous effect on the credit and currency position throughout the world.

There are two essential conditions, both of which must be fulfilled before reparation payments can be carried out. The first is that the debtor country shall be able to achieve in its government budget a surplus equal to the amount due. If it is unable to collect in taxation from its nationals such a surplus, it clearly will not have the wherewithal to pay. There seems no doubt that immediately after the war Germany was so exhausted and impoverished that its government was really unable to collect enough in taxation to meet internal expenses and at the same time satisfy the demands of the Allies. In its despair it had recourse to the printing press, and manufactured paper money which did not represent any real increase in the sum total of its national wealth but only wrecked its currency and ruined its investing classes.

But assuming that the government of a country has been able to accumulate a genuine surplus on its year's budget, this wealth can only be transferred to its creditors across the frontier on condition that the nation in its commercial and financial dealings with other nations has established a favourable balance of visible and invisible trade for that amount. Exports must have largely exceeded imports. The only alternative is that of the improvident debtor who goes on borrowing at usurious rates to pay current expenditure.

It will be recalled that these conditions were clearly stated by me in my reply to M. Doumer in January 1921, of which an account has already been given in Chapter V.

To complete the picture, I must add that as the European countries which are creditors on Germany for reparations are in turn debtors to the United States, in respect of purchases they made from her during the world conflict, the reparation payments made by Germany terminate partly in France—the chief creditor for reparations—and in Belgium, but mainly in the United States, whither they are passed by the ordinary operations of international finance, for settlement of war-debts. So in order to complete the reparation transaction, France and more particularly the United States

81

ought to be prepared to receive, each year, direct or indirect imports of German goods—mainly manufactured—unbalanced by corresponding exports of their own. By indirect imports, I mean that when some other country sells goods to America, the bill is paid by goods from Germany, instead of from the United States. While direct imports tend to displace by so much in the American home market the domestic products of her manufacturers, indirect imports forestall America's export trade in its customary foreign markets.

To set against these considerations there was, however, a general expectation abroad just after the war that a great revival and forward movement of peace-time industry and commerce would replace the intensive labours of war and munition production, and would busy itself with satisfying the need and demand which had accumulated during $4\frac{1}{2}$ years of war activity. Armies and armaments, and the old national fears and distrusts which had hampered the world in pre-war days and diverted so much of its energy to unproductive channels would become obsolete. All nations would co-operate in the eager progress of a new era.

Had such a development taken place, it was at least thinkable that amid the immensely increased industrial output and consumption of all countries, a considerable surplus of goods might be produced by Germany and absorbed by her creditors, which would yet not gravely injure either her credit or their employment.

But the event fell out otherwise. Though the peace treaties were signed, and a league of the nations was set up to keep the peace, some of the nations never abandoned their war-time mentality. The first reaction of every calamity is to create an intense desire to prevent its repetition, and to concentrate all thought and energy on that particular kind of disaster to the exclusion of all other possible or probable mishaps. The danger of that frame of mind is that it is apt to be neurotic and unbalanced and that its energies are mis-directed. It is haunted with the spectre of symptoms and secondary causes, and not with the root causes of the evil.

Instead of building bridges across their frontiers, and seeking to unite with their neighbours in a great common effort, based on mutual goodwill and aiming to achieve mutual benefit and progress, the frightened nations set to work to increase and perfect their armaments, and in international policy to cripple their former enemies and ring them with hostile States. Europe was thus doomed to a state of chaos and frustration from which we have not yet emerged, and in that welter all our hopes of swift industrial progress perished. A volume of reparation payments which Germany might, though only with much toil and trouble, have been able to devote out of her industrial earnings if peace and reconstruction had been the general policy of the world, and which the creditor nations might in turn have been able to receive from her without grave injury to their own flourishing industry and commerce, became a sum far beyond her capacity to furnish, or theirs to assimilate.

The post-war policy of France and her Allies on the Continent must therefore be regarded as one of the major causes directly responsible for Germany's failure to pay reparations. They had to choose between a policy of befriending Germany and encouraging her economic recovery to a level at which she would be able to pay; or one of weakening and shattering her in the presumed interests of their own future safety. Under M. Poincaré's influence they chose the second course, whilst expecting to reap the full benefit of the first. By the time the Ruhr adventure was concluded, all prospect of full reparation had disappeared.

Closely interlocking in its effects with this policy, and to some extent arising from the same mental attitude, was the system of high tariff barriers and other interferences with international trade which sprang up after the war, and is now strangling the world. Estimates of Germany's capacity to pay which were framed immediately after the war were naturally based to some extent on the figures of her pre-war trade. But circumstances proved to have changed very much, for large parts of the central empires had been cut off by the peace treaties and attached to their victors and to the new succession States. This not only reduced Germany's productive resources and sharply restricted her internal marketing area, but set up against her a new array of high customs frontiers, which these States vied with each other in raising. A wave of economic nationalism swept over the world—not confined to Europe—and everywhere there appeared new restrictions upon trade.

America in particular—the principal ultimate creditor in respect of those international war liabilities which reparations were used to settle—has since the war been raising ever higher and higher customs barriers up to the insurmountable wall of the Hawley-Smoot tariff. Rather than see German goods flood her domestic and export markets, America has lent Germany immense sums with which to pay her instalments, and actual payment has hitherto chiefly been made, not with goods, but with gold obtained by this borrowed money. Of the £650,000,000 (gold value) received by the United States and France for war-debts and reparations in the years 1922–1931, no less than £550,000,000 is represented by a net influx of gold into those two countries to that amount. This has practically exhausted the transferable gold available for such a purpose. Whereas at the end of 1913, the United States and France had between them 37.7 per cent of the world's monetary gold supplies, by June 30th, 1931, they had 61.7 per cent, or little short of two-thirds the total world supply. America's stock alone increased in this interval by over four thousand million dollars.

REPARATIONS AND WAR-DEBTS

The draining away of the world's gold supplies has made gold scarce and dear—which means that, by comparison with gold, all other property and goods have become cheap. The immense fall in the value of everything has bankrupted industry and finance. The money value (in gold) of investments, securities, stores, and the products of industry and agriculture has collapsed until it is no longer worth while commercially to make things or grow them for sale. Hence the world to-day is faced with that industrial stagnation and financial bankruptcy of which I have given illustrations in my introductory chapter.

With its industry and commerce at a standstill, America can no longer afford to go on lending Germany money to pay its reparation debts. Germany can no longer afford to borrow because the current interest on her external debts of all kinds is beyond her capacity to pay.

Germany has in recent years sunk immense sums in rationalizing her industries and renewing or reconditioning all her industrial plant and equipment, so as to be able to produce the goods with which alone she can ultimately settle her liabilities for reparations. But unless her creditors are willing to accept year by year an immense volume of these goods, at a good price, this increased production will never materialize in reparations. Indeed, while Germany's credit remains exhausted, she cannot even procure the raw materials with which to make goods to pay for the loans she has already received.

CHAPTER VIII

THE END OF REPARATIONS

The latest history of reparations demonstrates the full force of the considerations advanced in the previous chapter.

The Dawes Plan had left open the question of the total sum which Germany should ultimately be required to pay. This issue had deliberately been excluded from the terms of reference of the Dawes Committee, for M. Poincaré, who was in power in France when it was set up, would never have consented to letting such a body deal with that matter.

Yet it was impossible to drift on indefinitely without coming to a precise settlement of the question. The existence of this contingent liability for gigantic and undefined sums which hung over Germany was all the time impairing her credit. When she succeeded in borrowing it was at more and more crushing rates of interest. It was clear that unless something was done to remove this impending avalanche of indebtedness, Germany would soon be without any working capital to carry on her industries and earn the means to make reparation payments. While it had been policy just after the war to postpone the fixing of her total payments, lest they should be set too high, it was now possible to secure agreement for a more moderate figure, and necessary to do so, if future payments were to be forthcoming at all.

Accordingly in September 1928, a conference of the Allied governments met at Geneva and resolved to set up a committee of experts that should prepare a scheme for the final settlement of the reparation problem. This committee,

86

commonly spoken of as the "Young Committee," presented its report in June 1929.

Already it was apparent that further reductions would have to be made in the demands on Germany. Whereas the full annuity under the Dawes Plan had been fixed at 2,500,000,000 gold marks a year, the Young Plan set out a modulated scale of yearly payments, the average amount of which during the first 37 years was only 1,988,800,000, after which it declined for the remainder of the period, the final contemplated payment in 1987–88 being only 897,800,000.

There was good reason for this moderation on the part of the Young Committee; for since the inception of the Dawes Plan, Germany had not actually transferred any balances abroad. Up till 1929 she in effect made all her payments out of loans advanced to her by other countries. Her reparation payments in cash and kind from 1924 right up to the Hoover moratorium in 1931 totalled only £500,000,000, while during 1924–1930 inclusive her net balance of foreign indebtedness for loans made to her increased by £900,000,000—which included a net balance of indebtedness on short-term loans of £250,000,000. The Young Committee did not of course foresee how imminent was the collapse of this method of financing reparations; but this process of borrowing to pay current debts is bound sooner or later to land the debtor, and not infrequently the creditor, in a condition of inextricable financial embarrassment. The best thing that can happen to both is that the lender should stop his improvident loans before the borrower becomes hopelessly insolvent. It precipitates the crisis whilst there is some chance of handling it. That is what happened to Germany in 1931.

In the autumn of 1929 there was a disastrous break in the New York stock market, shortly to be followed by one in England; and thereafter the full tide of a world-wide depression gathered force and spread. In Central Europe this led to a drying up of the streams of loan money which hitherto had financed their industrial development and paid their external liabilities. Before long a movement arose to withdraw the short-term advances that had been made.

By mid-1931 the total debts of Germany to foreign investors stood at over 23,000,000,000 marks, and she could find no one able and willing to lend her any more money, even on the most usurious terms. As the charges for interest and repayment of these debts would eat up any external credit balance of trade that Germany could for the present achieve, it was clear that further reparation payments from her simply could not be obtained. Insistence upon such payments would not produce them; it would only involve Germany in open default and bankruptcy.

Such was the situation which produced the wise and courageous proposal of the United States President, Mr. Hoover, for a year's complete moratorium for all reparation and war-debt payments. War-debts had of course to be included in the scheme, for reparations were the ultimate source—in fact, one might almost say that in effect they were the immediate source—from which they were being paid. A moratorium was the only prompt means of averting the collapse of international credit and finance which would immediately have followed the open bankruptcy of Germany.

The benefits of the Hoover moratorium proposal were very nearly ruined by France's attitude. Thanks to the extent to which both Britain and the United States have cancelled their claims on France for war-debts, she is the next largest beneficiary after the United States in net balance of receipts from the settlement of reparations and war-debts. She was also less concerned than other countries in the liabilities which Germany had incurred to raise money for reparations. Of those loans less than 5 per cent had been contributed by France. She did not see why the United States, Britain,

REPARATIONS AND WAR-DEBTS

Holland and Switzerland, having already lent so much money to Germany, should not go on lending her more money with which to pay France. French unemployment was then a matter of a few almost negligible thousands. France was not in the least upset by the millions of American and British workless. Her statesmen who contemplated with such placid superiority the derelict workshops of the United States, Britain and Germany had not the vision to perceive that the clouds were gathering and already becoming visible on the French horizon. France was far more perturbed by the possible legal implications of a suspension of the Young Plan than she was by the prospect of Germany being driven to bankruptcy. It was only after long delay, and the agreement of the other countries to the staging of a formal if not farcical procedure for the payment by Germany into the Bank of International Settlements of the non-postponable annuities, and their immediate re-loan to her, that these legal objections were surmounted and the moratorium agreed. By that time a state of financial stress had been created which still holds Central Europe hanging halfway down the abyss.

Since then we have had the Report of the Young Plan Advisory Committee, which met at Basle in December 1931, nominally to advise whether Germany should be allowed to postpone payment of the "postponable" portion of the Young Plan annuities. The committee, for the appointment of which provision had been made in Articles 119 and 127 of the Young Plan, in the event of an application by Germany for such postponement, consisted of nominees of the national banks in the principal creditor countries—the representative from Britain being Sir Walter Layton, and the American representative, Dr. Walter W. Stewart. The committee not only concluded that such postponement would be inevitable, but took sufficient liberty with its terms of reference to include a survey of the whole economic position, and to utter

89

a warning that any resumption of these payments was highly problematical, and that therewith the whole tissue of war-debt arrangements had grown rotten. Reparations could not be paid, and in consequence the whole war-debt problem would take on a new aspect and require readjustment.

"The adjustment of all inter-governmental debts (reparations and other war-debts) to the existing troubled situation of the world—and this adjustment should take place without delay if new disasters are to be avoided—is the only lasting step capable of re-establishing confidence, which is the very condition of economic stability and real peace."

The report concluded with an earnest appeal to all the governments concerned "to permit of no delay in coming to decisions which will bring an amelioration of this grave crisis which weighs so heavily on all alike."

While by its terms of reference the Basle Committee was limited to considering the postponable portion of the Young Plan annuities, its report implies pretty clearly that it does not consider there is any prospect of even the unconditional payments being resumed when the Hoover moratorium expires at midsummer. Since then, Herr Brüning, the German Chancellor, has uttered a warning that Germany will not be able to resume payment. It is in fact most doubtful whether any German government could under present conditions retain office if it attempted to continue reparation payments. There is one factor which is beyond doubt—there is no country in the world whose bankers are prepared to resume the financing of Germany's interest payments on reparation account. That means definitely that Germany can no longer make these payments.

Whether there is or is not any possibility that arrangements could be made to save something out of the wreck, and secure at a future date a limited further payment from Germany, it is quite certain that on anything like the scale at which they have hitherto been assessed and exacted, German reparations are now dead.

I may add that in my view it is not worth while keeping afloat any part of the reparation debts. I am fully convinced that salvage operations to rescue any scrap from the deep into which it has sunk are not worth the cost and risk.

Their history, as it has been briefly summarized in the preceding pages, may have given readers the impression that very little has in fact been paid. This would be erroneous. The ledgers have been kept by the Allies and the principles of fair accountancy have been outraged in the way the debit and credit columns have been manipulated. Indeed, I feel certain that in no Allied country is there any adequate conception of the size of the contribution already made by Germany towards reparations. The actual amount of that contribution is a matter of some dispute, because of varying estimates of the value of the goods delivered by Germany in the period immediately after the war, and of the sums consumed by the oppressive charges of the occupation. But in any case, it was an immense payment for a defeated country, exhausted by a protracted war, stripped of territory, destitute of credit, and harassed by repeated interference, to produce.

The total payments made by or on account of Germany to the Allied and Associated Powers for reparation and cost of occupation from the Armistice to July 1st, 1931, when the Hoover moratorium came into force amounted, according to the estimate of the Reparation Committee, to £1,010,000,000. That is five times as large as the war indemnity paid to Germany by the French after 1871.

Germany herself estimates the value of her total payments in this period at a much higher figure, viz.: £2,695,000,000, while according to the computation of the Washington Institute of Economics in the United States of America—a calculation based on very careful investigation—the figure should be £1,905,000,000. This intermediate estimate, worked out by an independent and impartial authority, is probably the most accurate available.

It becomes less surprising that Germany has in practice found it impossible to pay a larger proportion of her total liability across her frontier when we remember that France, Belgium and Italy—to say nothing of Germany, Austria, and Russia—have failed to pay even their own nationals for moneys advanced by them to meet the cost of the war. The French franc has been stabilized at about one-fifth of its pre-war value, thus wiping out four-fifths of France's internal debt. The Belgian franc has been stabilized at one-seventh, wiping out six-sevenths of the Belgian debt, while in Italy, with the lira now stabilized at slightly over a fourth of its pre-war value, nearly three-quarters of the debt has been obliterated. Yet the demand is still made in quarters that have been driven to default in their payments to their own nationals, that Germany could be expected to pay twenty shillings in the pound across her frontier.

Were the total reparation liability of £6,600,000,000 which was originally imposed on Germany by the Reparation Commission paid by her in the same ratio as France has settled her internal war-debts—including the liability of France to thousands of British citizens who trustfully invested in the war-loan of their Ally—Germany would be required to pay not more than £1,350,000,000; if the American estimate of her actual payments to date be taken as correct, she would thus have already discharged considerably more than the whole burden. In either case she has already paid more than could be reasonably expected from her if we are to judge her by standards which French and Belgian governments have set up for their own solemn obligations to men and women of their own kith and kin.

While I am on this point, I may add that the proportion of her reparation debt which Germany has paid compares still more favourably with the payments which France has hitherto made on account of her war-debts. The total of the funded war-debts of France to Britain and the United States amounts to approximately £1,426,000,000. So far, she has paid less than £110,000,000 on these accounts, or about one-thirteenth of the sums owed.

Nor should it be forgotten that the reparation payments made by Germany are by no means the sole forfeit imposed on her. To illustrate the story of her losses, I will quote a graphic picture given by Herr von Kühlmann, formerly German Foreign Secretary, in his recent work: *Gedanken über Deutschland:*

"For nearly five years, Germany waged the greatest war in the history of the world, as the mainstay of a great coalition. Some of her Allies, such as Bulgaria and Turkey, were very inadequately equipped with ordnance factories. Some of them, like Austria-Hungary, were prevented from putting forth their whole strength through the hostile attitude of certain sections of their population (Czechs); others, like Turkey, were already exhausted through long years of warfare (the wars of Tripoli and the Balkans) when they entered the World War. This made it necessary for Germany to come to their aid in all directions, not only with leaders, troops and technicians, but also to the furthest possible extent with money, provisions and munitions of war. After an heroic resistance, in face of a blockade which grew ever closer, Germany was bound to find herself at the end of the World War thoroughly pumped dry. Her reserves of man-power were beaten down, her resources in every department eaten up in immense, heroically contested battles, and her nervous energy very largely exhausted.

"Upon this State, bled white in every respect, the commands of the Versailles Treaty were imposed. Germany lost about one-eighth of its territory, over 70,000 square kilometres with six-and-a-half million inhabitants. In the Saar basin and in Upper Silesia it was despoiled of a valuable part of its coal, immense supplies of iron ore and other metals, and a considerable area of its forests. Put into figures, there were taken away—to give just a few examples—16 per cent of the coal supplies it possessed in 1913; over 48 per cent of the iron ore; of its productive capacity for iron and steel about 20 per cent; and of its zinc ores 59 per cent.

"The whole of its colonial possessions were taken away.

"Of munitions of war it was compelled to hand over:

5,800,000 rifles and muskets
102,000 machine guns
28,000 trench mortars
53,000 field guns and heavy artillery
13,000 aëroplanes
24,000 aëroplane motors
50,000 ammunition wagons
55,000 military vehicles
11,000 field kitchens
1,150 field ovens
1,800 pontoons

Almost the whole of its supplies—running into many millions—of cartridges, shells, bombs, fuses, etc., and a vast amount of other war material.

"Its whole property and capital in foreign countries was confiscated or liquidated.

"The German sea cables were expropriated.

"On top of that, a war-debt amounting to 132 thousand million gold marks was imposed on Germany, in addition to

94

REPARATIONS AND WAR-DEBTS

a long array of deliveries in kind. Enormous quantities of railway materials, locomotives and wagons were handed over, likewise half the supplies in stock and a quarter of the subsequent production of dye-stuffs and chemical products; gigantic piles of timber, agricultural machinery and seeds, cattle and horses; compulsory deliveries of coal for long years to come.

"This far from complete list may give a picture of what was squeezed out from the exhausted land. The attempts to overtake the demands for reparations, and later the passive resistance in the Ruhr, brought about a time when the printing press spewed out bank-notes in insane confusion, which lost their purchasing value with every hour, until in November 1923 the dollar attained the astronomical rate of 4.2 billion marks, and therewith the old ramparts of the German realm were finally obliterated.

"Thus did this frightful war leave the unhappy nation bled white, without a government, without defence, stripped bare of capital, of all stores, and of all reserves."

This poignant extract is on the whole an incomplete narrative of what the peace terms and the bill for reparations have meant to Germany in the past. The worst chapters of the story are now being enacted.

CHAPTER IX

REPARATIONS AND WAR-DEBTS

Up to this point I have spoken mainly of the post-war liability of Germany to the Allied and Associated Powers to make payment for war damages inflicted by her. But this was not the only international liability created by the war. In addition, there were the debts owed by the Allies to one another and to their associate, the United States, in respect of supplies of munitions of war, foodstuffs, etc. Among the Powers opposed to Germany there was a considerable variation as regards their internal resources for the equipment and provisioning of their armies in the field. There was also a marked difference in their financial capacity to buy abroad what they could not produce for themselves.

We in Britain are even in peace-time largely dependent on overseas purchases for our food and raw materials. During the war we also bough' munitions and other supplies for our use from the United ^tes and elsewhere—and paid for them. And we furnished s pplies on an extensive scale to our Allies. As the war went 1, some of our Allies who were also buying abroad but not paying, found their credit exhausted, and we stepped in and covered their purchases with our guarantee, or sold them on credit goods we had already available, such as steel, replacing them with purchases on our own credit from America.

Objections have been raised in some quarters against the statement that our American debt was incurred on behalf of our Allies, on the ground that only a small part of it arose

REPARATIONS AND WAR-DEBTS

explicitly from guarantees given by us to the United States in respect of credits advanced by her to our Allies. But this small technical argument is an attempt to ignore the broad fact of these transactions. Had our Allies been able to pay us for the goods we supplied to them, we should never have incurred a halfpenny of debt to America, for the payments due to us from Europe would have been set against our liabilities to the United States for purchases we made from her, and settled in the ordinary course of business by the clearing-house methods of international finance, leaving us very much to the good.

As, however, we were compelled to finance our Allies on a very considerable scale, the position reached by the end of the war was that we had contracted a big debt to America, which was, however, less than half the total sum owed to us by our Allies. In round figures, we owed the United States £840,000,000 while our Allies owed us £1,950,000,000. If from this last figure we exclude the loans we had made to Russia during the war, we were still creditors for £1,300,000,000—leaving us in a net creditor position as regards war-debts to the tune of £460,000,000, apart from reparations due. If to this is added Britain's share of the reparation debt, the balance due to us was much more considerable.

It is very difficult to state fairly and candidly the facts which influence European opinion on this delicate question of contractual debts between nations without provoking resentments. All the same, candour is essential if we are to arrive at wise conclusions in the interests alike of creditors and debtors. I will do my best to narrate the facts in such a way as will avoid giving offence to men of good-will in every country.

From the outset Britain, although she was more creditor than debtor, took the view that the best course with all these war-debts was to cancel them. They were a paper record of inter-governmental transactions in the course of our great common effort for victory, on behalf of which all nations engaged had poured forth their blood and treasure. I have always felt that during the war the Allies ought to have been readier to pool their resources of men and munitions of war. Had they done so Russia, Serbia and Roumania would not have collapsed. Italy and the Danubian Powers with the help of Russia, had their armies been as well equipped as those of France and Britain, would have crushed Austria, and the war would have been over in 1917. Germany, unpropped and unprotected on her southern front, could not have maintained her redoubtable fight. What a difference that would have made to the world! Unfortunately each army established proprietary rights in its own front and each of them developed its own claim with such capital and equipment as it had at its disposal, and at no period of the war did the Allied Powers make the best use of their overwhelming superiority in men and material—certainly not until the last year of the war. During that year the policy of pooling resources not only gave us a real unity of command, but it enabled the Allies to equip the American troops with light and heavy artillery, aëroplanes and other essentials, and thus gave, without loss of time, the full benefit to the Allied cause of the valour of those fine soldiers from the great Republic.

To apply a commercial foot-rule to the measurement of our comparative sacrifices in human life would be, obviously, intolerable. Hardly less unseemly was it to treat as business liabilities the material assistance which one ally had been forced to accept from another in the desperate ferocity of a struggle to avoid a defeat which would have brought disaster to ally and associate alike.

That was our view, openly expressed in reference to these inter-Allied war-debts; but it was not the view the United

States took of the matter. She was by the end of the war an even larger creditor for war-debts than we, having lent altogether rather more than £2,000,000,000 to her associates in Europe, who had borne the burden of devastation and carnage of the war for three-and-a-half years before the United States came in. In every other respect it must be admitted that her contribution to the common cause was very much less. She had kept out of the war altogether for three years, during which time she had enjoyed undisturbed the world markets in which she had formerly competed for business with the industrialists of Europe; and she had done a flourishing and highly profitable trade in munitions and supplies for the Allies, for much of which she had been paid in cash. Even after her entry into the war, this trade continued at a brisk pace. While the total number of British troops who lost their lives in the World War was 743,702 (excluding Dominion and Colonial troops) and that of the French was 1,385,300, the number for the United States was 115,660. The cost of her participation in the Great War, according to the estimate of the Bankers' Trust Company of New York and Paris, involved for the United States an expenditure of 8.67 per cent of her national wealth. For Great Britain it involved 34.39 per cent.

I am the last man to minimize the incalculable aid the strength of this mighty land brought to the Allies. I was Prime Minister at the time America came into the war and I have a grateful recollection of the relief their accession brought to the hard-pressed Allies. America came in after the breakdown of Russia, the elimination of Roumania and the conquest of Serbia by the Germanic forces. The Allies were not even holding their own and the issue was in doubt. America settled it. She converted a stalemate into victory.

All the same, I am certain that every American citizen will readily acknowledge that the United States did not from first

99

to last make any sacrifice or contribution, remotely comparable to those of her European associates, in life, limb, money, material or trade, towards the victory which she shared with them. Even the total cancellation of the war-debts due to her by them would not bring her contribution up to anything approaching a comparable burden in money alone.

Speaking on this subject, the American commander, General Pershing, has said:

"If it had not been that the Allies were able to hold the lines for fifteen months after we had entered the war, hold them with the support of the loans we made, the war might well have been lost. We scarcely realized what those loans meant to them and to us.

"It seems to me that there is some middle ground where we should bear a certain part of the expense in maintaining the Allied armies on the front while we were preparing, instead of calling all this money a loan and insisting upon its repayment. We were responsible. We gave the money knowing it would be used to hold the Boche until we could prepare. Fifteen months! Think of it."

The United States, however, became highly irate at the faintest hint of cancellation. The debts, she insisted, must be duly paid; paid to the uttermost farthing—though in her eventual settlements with some of her debtors (except Britain) she moderated somewhat this extreme attitude. If in their handling of the question of German reparations the Allies seemed to be at times rather harshly insistent, it must be borne in mind that they in turn were under liabilities to the United States, whose attitude to her debtors was still more unbending.

In some quarters it is asserted that there is no similarity between reparations and war-debts, and no logical connection between them. Such a view may be all very well for the theorist. But in solid reality and in practical experience, these two forms of liability are closely similar and vitally connected.

Both reparations and war-debts were liabilities incurred as the inevitable result of military operations. They are both inseparable from war. They did not represent in either case the bill for solid additions to its national capital which had been received by the debtor country. Indeed, Germany and the Allies were alike in being poorer after they had incurred these liabilities than before, by reason of the very exertions which had caused their debts to be incurred. And it may be added that except perhaps in the case of the British debt to America, the liabilities with which the belligerent countries were saddled by the end of the war far exceeded their capacity to pay in full across their frontiers, or even—so far as their internal debts were concerned—to repay to their own nationals. In their practical aspect as international liabilities, war-debts and reparations were on all fours.

As to the working connection of reparations and war-debts, it is enough to point out that the advances made by their creditors to the debtor countries were for the purpose of aiding them to victory, and were used up on the field of battle for that end. Victory itself was not an asset which could be cashed in payment of the debts, and the only material asset reaped from the conflict was the prospect of reparations. True, these were in theory only reparations for damages, not an indemnity; but as no additional sum for indemnity would have been forthcoming even if demanded, the name mattered little. Viewed commercially, had the war been a business undertaking on the part of the Allies, reparations were the sole marketable asset accruing from their operations, so that the investors in the business would have had to look to reparations as the sole source from which dividends or repayment of the capital invested would be forthcoming. As a matter of historical fact, all repayments of war-debts actually made by the Allies (except the earlier payments by Great Britain to America) have been made out of their receipts from reparations.

It is urged that the victorious countries have been compensated and enriched by the addition to their empires across the seas of vast territories in Africa and elsewhere, which were formerly colonies of the German Empire. The African Colonies and Palestine were offered to America and she refused them on the ground that her experience in the Philippines did not lead her to the conclusion that annexations of remote territories were an asset. On the contrary, she was convinced that they constituted a burden and a worry. The American delegates for that reason adopted a more astute device—that of the mandates. All the conquered territories of Germany overseas (with a few exceptions which were contiguous to the Dominions and were definitely annexed by them) were handed over to the League of Nations which in turn gave a revocable mandate in respect of those colonies to the Great Powers. These mandates were conditional upon the open door for world trade. Britain, France and Belgium had the responsibility and the cost but the United States shared to the full all trading advantages. Britain has already surrendered her full Mesopotamian mandate after spending scores of millions to restore order out of chaos and to start an independent Arab kingdom with something like a good chance of making good.

At the Peace Conference, America would enter into no discussion as to any reduction in the figure of Allied debts to her, though she was urgent that the formulation of the Allies' claims for reparations should be kept within Germany's capacity to pay. Yet she could hardly expect much response to this plea, while her rulers were at the same time protesting their determination to collect in full from comrades-in-arms the debts they owed to her, without any corresponding modification of the total on the basis of their capacity to pay. If Germany had been exhausted by the war, so had the Allies. In addition, they had suffered the full devastation of the war, since it had been fought over their territory, while Germany remained unscathed.

Mr. Bernard M. Baruch, the able economic adviser to the American delegation, and American member of the Reparation Commission, admits in his book on the subject that the separation of inter-Allied debts and reparations left the Allies in a position to urge in reply to the American proposals:

"If you ask us to lessen our claims upon Germany for indemnity, which she admits she owes, what will you do for the war loan you made to us for the prosecution of a war which was as much your war as our war, the amount of which clearly exceeds our capacity to pay unless we are allowed to get the last possible dollar out of Germany?"*

If America insists upon the redemption by the Allied countries of the full amount of their funded debts, she will have exacted a larger war indemnity from her friends who fought her battle as well as their own, than the Allies are ever likely to exact from their late enemies.

Great Britain has no reason to be ashamed of the attitude she adopted in face of this issue. We were on balance a large creditor nation. The amounts due to us from our Allies and from German reparations totalled four times as much as the debt we had incurred to the United States. Even excluding German reparations, and the immense bad debt owed to us by Russia, we were owed by our Allies more than half as much again as our debt to America. Yet we took from the

*The Making of the Reparation & Economic Sections of the Treaty, p. 52.

outset the view that all inter-Allied debts should be wiped out, and that the financial contributions of the victors, no less than their military contributions, should be regarded as having been paid into a common pool for the achievement of victory. In his book on *Woodrow Wilson and World Settlement*, Mr. R. S. Baker, an eminent member of President Wilson's administration, states that hints were made from the British side to the United States Government as early as December 1918, of the desirability of an all-round cancellation of the inter-Allied war-debts. But he adds that these hints

"had been promptly discouraged and were not revived in express terms until toward the close of 1919. But this question of the debts hung constantly over the conference, as it has hung over the world ever since, as one demanding a bold solution if the financial rehabilitation of the nations was to be at all thorough-going."

From the outset of the Peace Conference, this rigid attitude of the United States on the subject of war-debts made any concession on reparations exceedingly difficult. Thus Mr. Baker writes:

"The committee (a sub-committee of the Commission on Reparations) was limited, at the start, by the position of the United States Government. While on the one hand President Wilson had declared himself immovably against the inclusion of war costs in the claims against Germany, on the other, the United States Treasury had flatly refused to consider any re-adjustment of the European debts to us. While Americans always insisted that these debts had nothing to do with reparations or rehabilitation, the Europeans were equally sure that the connection was vital. On March 1st . . . the financial drafting committee . . . presented a report in which the first subject set down for reference to a financial commission was this:

"'Inter-Allied agreements as to the consolidation, re-apportionment, re-assumption of war-debts.'

"The United States Treasury pounced upon the challenge it felt to lie in the very mention of this subject. In notes of March 8th to the French and Italian commissioners at Washington, it declared that 'The Treasury. . . . will not assent to any discussion at the Peace Conference, or elsewhere, of any plan or arrangement for the release, consolidation, or re-apportionment of the obligations of foreign governments held by the United States.'"

These extracts from American sources show at once the intimate connection which has from the first been recognized to subsist between war-debts and reparations, and the extreme tenacity with which President Wilson and his advisers refused to acknowledge officially this connection, even though the refusal stultified any effort made by them to bring about a peace settlement that would permit an early recovery of Europe from its dislocation and distress.

On April 23rd, 1919, whilst the Peace Conference was sitting, I wrote to President Wilson, sending him a copy of Professor Keynes' financial plan for the economic rehabilitation of Europe. This plan provided for a huge bond issue by the ex-enemy Powers and the new States that had been constituted in whole or part out of their territories. The bonds were to be guaranteed by the Allies and by neutral Powers, and of their proceeds, four-fifths were to be applied to the payment of reparations and one-fifth left available for the purchase of raw materials for use by the issuing States. These bonds, moreover, were to be acceptable at par "in payment of all indebtedness between any of the Allied and associated governments." This plan would in effect have wiped out the bulk of inter-Allied indebtedness by liquidating it with the bonds delivered for reparations. Any failure by Germany subsequently to honour these bonds to the full would have made the loss fall chiefly on the richer guaranteeing nations—the United States and Britain, and would have the same effect as a cancellation by them and us of so much of the war-debts due to us.

My covering letter to the President said:

"Apart from private enterprise, His Majesty's Government see only two possible courses—direct assistance and various forms of guaranteed finance, on a very much larger scale than is at present contemplated, by the more prosperous of the Allied and associated countries, which probably means to an extent of not less than 90 per cent, the United States; or an attempt to recreate the credit system of Europe and by some form of world-wide co-operation to enable the countries whose individual credit is temporarily destroyed to trade on their prospects of reparation from enemy States or to capitalize their future prospects of production. Every consideration of policy and interest indicates the superiority of the second . . .

"The scheme is an attempt to deal simultaneously in as simple a way as possible with several distinct problems. . . . The acute problem of the liquidation of inter-ally indebtedness, while not disposed of, is sensibly ameliorated . . ."

In his reply, dated May 3rd, 1919, to my letter, President Wilson declined to consider the scheme, stating that America could neither undertake to guarantee such bonds, nor to furnish capital for the economic reinstatement of Europe; and that reparations did not furnish a good security, since by withdrawing Germany's working capital they would prevent her from earning the wherewithal to make further payments. I may point out, in passing, that America's refusal to contemplate some such plan landed her in practice in the other and worse alternative of indiscriminate lending to Europe. In partciular, her loans to Germany had by June 30th, 1931 (when the Hoover moratorium came into force) mounted to over 8,400,000,000 gold marks, and she was carrying more than 55 per cent of the total long-term loans which Germany had succeeded in raising since the war.

I sent an answer to President Wilson on June 26th, 1919. In the course of my reply I reminded him that the United Kingdom had incurred war-debts, internal and external, totalling over $8\frac{1}{2}$ thousand million pounds, including the large debt to the United States; and that while our Allies owed us more than we owed the States, it was very doubtful how much they could hope to pay us. Meantime, the burden of debt per head borne by us had risen from £14 pre-war to £160.

"Britain," I said, "has already bled itself white for the sake of the Allies. It asks for nothing which is impossible, but it does claim that it has the right to ask its colleagues of the Peace Conference both to compel Germany to pay whatever she is capable of paying, and to place their own credit unreservedly at the disposal of the nations for the regeneration of the world as Great Britain placed hers unreservedly at the service of the Allies in order to save the freedom of the world."

But no appeal was of any avail to induce the President to co-operate practically in the urgent task of the economic reconstruction of Europe. It was at that time impossible to obtain outside of Britain any intelligent agreement among leading statesmen as to the need for such efforts. In treating of the story of reparations I have already shown what extraor-

107.

dinary limitations bounded the vision of responsible men as to the elementary facts of the international financial problem.

On August 5th, 1920, I wrote to President Wilson on a number of international issues. In the course of that letter I said:

"I now come to the other question I wish to write to you about, and that is the knotty problem of inter-Allied indebtedness. . . . The British and French governments have been discussing during the past four months the question of giving fixity and definiteness to Germany's reparation obligations. The British Government has stood steadily by the view that it was vital that Germany's liabilities should be fixed at a figure which it was within the reasonable capacity of Germany to pay, and that this figure should be fixed without delay because the reconstruction of Central Europe could not begin nor could the Allies themselves raise money on the strength of Germany's obligation to pay them reparation until her liabilities had been exactly defined. After great difficulties with his own people, M. Millerand found himself able to accept this view—but he pointed out that it was impossible for France to agree to accept anything less than it was entitled to under the Treaty unless its debts to its Allies and associates in the war were treated in the same way.

"This declaration appeared to the British Government eminently fair. But after careful consideration they came to the conclusion that it was impossible to remit any part of what was owed to them by France except as part and parcel of an all-round settlement of inter-Allied indebtedness. I need not go into the reasons which led to this conclusion, which must be clear to you. But the principal reason was that *British public opinion would never support a one-sided arrangement at its sole expense,* and that if such a one-sided arrangement were made it could not fail to estrange and eventually embitter the relations between the American and the British people with calamitous results to the future of the world. You will remember that Great Britain borrowed from the United States about half as much as its total loans to the Allies, and that after America's entry into the war, it lent to the Allies almost exactly the same amount as it borrowed from the United States. Accordingly the British Government has informed the French Government that it will agree to any equitable arrangement for the reduction or cancellation of inter-Allied indebtedness, but that such an arrangement must be one which applies all round. As you know, the representatives of the Allies and of Germany are meeting at Geneva in a week or two to commence discussion on the subject of reparation. . . .

"There is one other point which I should like to add. When the British Government decided that it could not deal with the question of the debts owed to it by its Allies except as part and parcel of any all-round arrangement of inter-Allied debts, the Chancellor of the Exchequer told Mr. Rathbone that he could not proceed any further with the negotiations which they had been conducting together with regard to the postponement of the payment of interest on the funding of Great Britain's debts to America. I should like to make it plain that this is due to no reluctance on the part of Great Britain to fund its debt, *but solely to the fact that it cannot bind itself by any arrangement which would prejudice the working of any inter-Allied arrangement which may be reached in the future.* If some method can be found for funding the British debt which does not prejudice the larger question, the British Government would be glad to fall in with it."

To this letter President Wilson replied on November 3rd, 1920. After assuring me that: "While you may at times have been fighting alone in the Supreme Allied Council for a liberal, just and constructive interpretation of the German Treaty, you have had, and I am sure can count upon having the support of the United States in such a policy," he proceeded, on the question of war-debts, to state:

"It is highly improbable that either the Congress or popular opinion in this country will ever permit a cancellation of any part of the debt of the British Government to the United States in order to induce the British Government to remit, in whole or in part, the debt to Great Britain of France or any other of the Allied Governments, or that it would consent to a cancellation or reduction in the debts of any of the Allied Governments as an inducement towards a practical settlement of the reparation claims."

This statement reads a little quaintly to-day in view of the fact that America has in fact remitted since then a large part of the debts due to her by France and Italy, though insisting on full payment from Britain.

In February 1922, the American Congress passed an act setting up the World War Foreign Debt Commission, and thereupon the United States Government officially requested debtor countries to take the necessary steps for funding their debts.

Up to this point, Britain had been practising its avowed preference for the policy of wiping out inter-Allied indebtedness all round by refraining from any demand upon the Allies who owed it money. We did not even press for the payment of interest on their debt, although our tax-payers were paying interest to British bankers on the money lent to the Allies, at the rate of 5 per cent. In face, however, of the American attitude, we were now compelled to approach our Allies and to point out to them that since America demanded payment from us we must in turn require at least a part payment from them.

REPARATIONS AND WAR-DEBTS

Accordingly a note was drafted by me, submitted to and agreed by the Cabinet—Sir Robert Horne, who has in more recent times voiced his disagreement in letters to the press, may have done so at that date. The note was then sent by Lord Balfour, as Acting Foreign Secretary, to the diplomatic representatives of our European debtors: France, Italy, Yugo-Slavia, Roumania, Portugal and Greece. This note, which has passed into history as the "Balfour Note," pointed out that although the British Government occupied a strongly creditor position, being owed altogether four times as much as it in turn owed to the United States, it would be prepared, "if such a policy formed part of a satisfactory international settlement, to remit all the debts due to Great Britain by our Allies in respect of loans, or by Germany in respect of reparations."

We expressed our regret that we were being driven off this policy by America's insistence on repayment of our debt to her.

"His Majesty's Government . . . cannot treat the repayment of the Anglo-American loan as if it were an isolated incident in which only the United States of America and Great Britain had any concern. It is but one of a connected series of transactions, in which this country appears sometimes as debtor, sometimes as creditor, and if our undoubted obligations as a debtor are to be enforced, our not less undoubted rights as a creditor cannot be left wholly in abeyance. . . . For evidently the policy hitherto pursued by this country of refusing to make demands upon its debtors is only tolerable so long as it is generally accepted. It cannot be right that one partner in the common enterprise should recover all that she has lent, and that another, while recovering nothing, should be required to pay all that she has borrowed. . . .

"The policy favoured by His Majesty's Government is, as I have already observed, that of surrendering their share of

111

German reparation, and writing off, through one great transaction, the whole body of inter-Allied indebtedness. But if this be found impossible of accomplishment, we wish it to be understood that we do not in any event desire to make a profit of any less satisfactory arrangement. In no circumstances do we propose to ask more from our debtors than is necessary to pay to our creditors . . ."

The principle then laid down, that this country would renounce every penny of the sums due to her from her Allies and from Germany, so far as her own profit was concerned, and would collect only so much as she was in turn compelled to pass over to America, has been faithfully adhered to in the arrangements we have subsequently made with our debtors. So loyally, indeed, have we observed it that we at present are in the paradoxical position, for the second largest creditor nation on war account, of being the only one of the victors which has paid more than it received. We have actually paid out £133,700,000 more than our total receipts from reparations and war-debts, whereas France has received £163,300,000 more than it has paid, and all the other Allies similarly have balances on the right side.

In view of the fact that the principle of the Balfour Note is now almost universally approved in this country, it is interesting to recall that on its first appearance its reception at home and abroad was discouraging. In Britain the attitude of the press was complicated by considerations of political hostility to the Government of the day.

It was not a propitious moment for the Government to put forward a great project of international appeasement. Politicians of all colours and shades were engaged in an intrigue much more congenial to their tastes, the restoration of party alignments. The Government of the day was a non-party administration called together to deal with the emergency of war and of the most urgent post-war problems. As the crisis receded the binding effect of national apprehension weakened and the power of the Ministry consequently waned. It is the fate of all non-party combinations. After the first fraternal impulse is exhausted, these coalitions are assailed by a variety of conflicting ambitions, partisan and personal, which they must needs leave unsatisfied. On the other hand, they command no party loyalties to defend or support them. It is not the interest of any individual party to advertise their successes or excuse their failures, because no party can profit by the former and the latter cannot be imputed to any single party.

In August 1922 the converging assault on the Government was about to reach its objective. The mines were all laid for blowing it up; it was only necessary to apply the match. You could hardly expect men whose whole energies had been absorbed in these manœuvres to be diverted at such a moment by thoughts about a world menace which could not bring catastrophe to the nations for some years and might never do so if the right persons were called in to handle affairs. So the Balfour Note was received with frigid indifference and occasional outspoken hostility at home; abroad America would have none of it, and the Prime Minister of France flung it back with an insult to the country that had issued it. Now that its proposals are being revived on all hands by bankers, industrialists, and journalists after their failure to give timely acceptance to it has brought unparalleled calamity to every country throughout the world, including our own, I can find no one who has the magnanimity to acknowledge the origin of the plan or to express any regret that he had not the wisdom to support it in good time.

The city was apathetic and financiers who now clamour for cancellation gave no support to our proposals. The city rarely sees beyond the next Contango. Every bank chairman has recently made cancellation the theme of his annual speech to shareholders, but in 1922 I do not recall that any leading banker expressed approval of the note or betrayed the slightest cognizance of the issue. As at the Peace Conference, so now, it was the politicians and the economists who took the longer view, and the practical business men and financiers who nurtured fantastic hopes of the wealth to be extracted from an exhausted Central Europe.

One or two critics urged that we should take the initiative by announcing that we were prepared to cancel debts due to us without any conditions as to how we were to be treated by our creditors. Events were quickly to undeceive those who had suggested we ought to have gone further, declaring that unconditional cancellation by us would have provoked other countries to an equal burst of generosity. On the contrary, the broad-minded view expressed by us met with no response elsewhere. The United States did not swerve from its extreme attitude of demanding the last farthing of the debts payable to it. As for France, the reply sent by M. Poincaré to the note makes perfectly amazing reading.

In his letter, dated September 1st, 1922, M. Poincaré maintained—as America was doing—that there was no connection between reparations and Allied debts. But there was this difference between their views, that while America insisted that war-debts must in any case be paid in full, whether reparations were forthcoming or not, M. Poincaré asserted that until reparations had been fully paid there could be no question of settling the war-debts.

I quote the following passages from his letter:

"If the Allied Governments had not afforded one another the reciprocal financial aid, out of which arose the war-debts, either the war would have ended badly for them or it would have lasted longer, and in any case it is the lending countries which should have made, either by the work of their industries or by the despatch of larger effectives, the effort which the borrowing countries made in their stead. . . .

"The German Reparation Debt is the result of wilful destruction, most of which was useless, and of the payment of pensions devolving on the Allied Governments for the losses inflicted by Germany. This necessary reparation of the damage wrought must naturally have priority over all other settlement. As far as France is concerned . . . there can be no question for her of contemplating any settlement of the debts she contracted during the war, so long as the outlay made by her, and still to be made, for the reconstruction of her devastated regions has not been covered by Germany directly, or by means of a transaction, which would allow her to mobilize as soon as possible an adequate portion of her debt.

"Once Germany has acquitted herself of this obligation, which must take precedence over all others, the French Government would not be opposed to the consideration of a general settlement of international debts. . . .

"Further, when the French Government comes to consider in particular settlement of her debt to Great Britain, certain considerations will first have to be taken into account. . . .

"When the payments made for the reconstruction of the devastated regions of France allow of a settlement of inter-Allied debts, such settlement will have to be preceded by a minute examination, in order to fix the amount of the debt at an equitable figure. . . ."

It will be seen that in general effect M. Poincaré's petulant and ill-conditioned letter was an assertion that France would pay no debts until the reparations had been forthcoming in full; that we had been slack and ineffective in our war effort; and that we had been guilty of sharp practice in our price

115

estimates for the munitions and other goods we had supplied to France.

This, be it noted, was his reply to our declaration that we were anxious to cancel all debts due to us, including French debts; that we would in any case cancel the bulk of them, and would not demand a penny piece for ourselves out of whatever settlement was ultimately reached!

A few weeks after this I vacated the office of Prime Minister. Mr. Bonar Law, who succeeded me, sent Mr. Stanley Baldwin and Mr. Montagu Norman to the United States in January 1923 to open negotiations for the funding of the British debt.

It was a bad combination. No worse team could have been chosen. Mr. Montagu Norman is the high priest of the golden calf and his main preoccupation was to keep his idol burnished and supreme in the Panthéon of commerce. In his honest view it was the only god to lead the nation out of the wilderness. Such a person was a dangerous counsellor for a man of Mr. Baldwin's equipment.

As to the two leading negotiators, Mr. Mellon and Mr. Baldwin, Mr. Mellon was keen, experienced, hard, ruthless; Mr. Baldwin casual, soft, easy-going, and at that time quite raw. Mr. Baldwin admits that since then he has learnt a great deal. At that time he merited his constant boast that he was only a "simple countryman." A business transaction at that date between Mr. Mellon and Mr. Baldwin was in the nature of a negotiation between a weasel and its quarry. The result was a bargain which has brought international debt collection into disrepute.

This was not because Mr. Baldwin was inadequately briefed, nor because he did not understand his brief. In fact, he showed in his first speech at these negotiations that he had been well coached as to the facts and possessed a thoroughly intelligent appreciation of them, as the following extracts from that speech clearly demonstrate:

"This debt is not a debt for dollars sent to Europe. The money was all expended here, most of it for cotton, wheat, food products and munitions of war. Every cent used for the purchase of these goods was spent in America; American labour received the wages; American capitalists the profits; the United States Treasury the taxation imposed on those profits.

"At the time these goods were bought, we were associated in a great war. Out of 7,000,000,000 dollars' worth of goods bought after the United States came into the war, we paid for 3,000,000,000 dollars, leaving 4,000,000,000 dollars which were supplied on credit. Now, seeing that the debt is a debt for goods supplied, it would be natural to ask, why not repay with goods?

"A moment's consideration is sufficient to answer that question.

"Those goods were supplied in war time at war prices. Prices have fallen so far that thus to repay 4,000,000,000 dollars, Great Britain would have to send America a far greater bulk of goods than she originally purchased with the money loaned, and laying aside all consideration of the tariff barrier, would it be possible for America to accept repayment in coal, steel, iron, manufactured cotton goods and so forth, a method of repayment which would affect the employment of her people for years to come?

". . . May I put it in this way? We intend to pay—but how can international credits be made liquid when the creditor nation is unwilling to permit liquidation through the direct delivery of goods and is also unwilling to see the current sale of her products to the debtor nation interrupted, and when the debtor nation is unwilling to be put in the position of being unable to buy the products of the creditor nation?"

REPARATIONS AND WAR-DEBTS

Yet it is a matter of familiar and painful history that in the course of these negotiations Mr. Baldwin proceeded, contrary to his instructions and in the teeth of the most express protests of his chief, to fix the terms of a most onerous settlement. He was backed in this by Lord Cave, and in the end Mr. Bonar Law gave in to the settlement—mainly because he did not want to split the Government so soon after its formation, when the Conservatives had only just got into power again for the first time for seventeen years. But on the last occasion when I ever saw Mr. Bonar Law before his death, at a luncheon given by a mutual friend, he told us how much he regretted that he had not insisted on resigning sooner than approve the terms which Mr. Baldwin had arranged.

The following figures may serve to illustrate the nature of this settlement.

Altogether, Great Britain borrowed from the United States during and just after the war sums amounting to 4,277,000,000 dollars, of which she repaid just over 202,000,000, leaving nearly 4,075,000,000 dollars standing as a debt.

The notes on which these sums were borrowed carried nominally interest at the rate of 5 per cent. When, however, the question of debt settlement arose, it had fairly to be pointed out that this rate was far too high for a duly funded debt by one government to another, and much higher than the interest rate at which the United States Government had actually raised, by its Liberty Bonds, the sums it had lent.

At the time when the Baldwin settlement was made, the United States Government was easily able to raise money at $3\frac{1}{2}$ per cent and Mr. Mellon, Secretary of the United States Treasury, subsequently stated that over the sixty-two years during which repayment was being spread out, the average cost of money to the United States Government would be only 3 per cent.

REPARATIONS AND WAR-DEBTS

Since America never admitted any suggestion of a reduction to Great Britain in the principal of the debt, negotiations could only affect the rate of interest and the period over which repayment should be spread out. As to these matters, the settlement arranged by Mr. Baldwin provided that the principal outstanding, together with accumulated interest at 4¼ per cent, should be funded and repaid over a period of sixty-two years together with interest at an average rate of 3.3 per cent throughout the period.

Already, in the autumn of 1922, we had paid over 100,000,000 dollars on account of interest outstanding, and we paid a further 4,000,000 odd at the time of funding, to leave a round sum of 4,600,000,000 dollars as our funded debt. The half-yearly instalments of principal and interest which we have contracted to pay in liquidation of this will in the course of the sixty-two years amount to a total of 11,105,965,000 dollars.

On the strength of the fact that the interest rates charged were below the original, purely nominal, figure of 5 per cent borne by the obligations we had furnished, it is commonly stated that America made a partial cancellation of the British debt. But in the light of Mr. Mellon's statement as to the actual cost of money to the United States Government, it may be urged that in fact we are overpaying. On the basis of a rate of interest of 3 per cent, the payments we contracted to make to the United States corresponded to a capital sum of 4,922,702,000 dollars—an overpayment of 7 per cent.

This settlement which Mr. Baldwin so hastily concluded staggered Europe. It amazed the business community of America. It was so unexpected. The Treasury officials were not exactly bluffing, but they put forward their full demand as a start in the conversations, and to their surprise Mr. Baldwin said he thought the terms were fair, and accepted them. If all business was as easy as that there would be no joy in its pursuit. But this crude job, jocularly called a "settlement," was to have a disastrous effect upon the whole further course of negotiations on international war-debts. The United States could not easily let off other countries with more favourable terms than she had exacted from us, and as a consequence the settlement of their American debts by our European Allies hung fire for years, provoking continual friction and bitterness. Equally the exorbitant figure we had promised to pay raised by so much the amounts which under the policy of the Balfour Note we were compelled to demand from our own debtors. Not alone Britain, but all Europe has suffered ever since from Mr. Baldwin's vicarious generosity.

Ultimately the United States agreed to fund the debts to her of our Continental Allies on terms markedly more favourable than she had granted to Britain. She reduced the rates of interest charged, not only on the funded debt, but also in respect of the accumulation of unpaid interest prior to funding. The following table shows the amount of the funded debts to the United States of Great Britain, Belgium, France, Yugo-Slavia and Italy, the total sums each of these countries was required under its settlements to pay in sixty-two years, and the rate of interest charged:

COUNTRY.	FUNDED DEBT.	TOTAL PAYMENTS IN 62 YEARS.	RATE OF INTEREST CHARGED.
	Dollars.	*Dollars.*	*Per cent.*
Britain	4,600,000,000	11,105,965,000	3.3
Belgium	417,780,000	727,830,500	1.8
France	4,025,000,000	6,847,674,104	1.6
Yugo-Slavia	62,850,000	95,177,635	1.0
Italy	2,042,000,000	2,407,677,500	0.4

REPARATIONS AND WAR-DEBTS

This table shows clearly the amazing discrepancy between the terms which the United States insisted upon in the case of Great Britain and those which she was content to accept from the other Allied Powers. We are expected to pay a total sum amounting to considerably more than twice our original debt. Nothing like this is demanded from these other countries. Yet we are at the same time the only one receiving nothing whatever on balance from the international repayment of war-debts and reparations. As I have already pointed out, we were in the position, at the time when the Hoover moratorium came into force, of having paid out £133,700,000 more than we had received in respect of war-debts and reparations; whereas these transactions had provided a net surplus of £118,800,000 to Belgium, £163,300,000 to France, £35,000,000 to Yugo-Slavia, and £28,000,000 to Italy.

I cannot help saying that I think in this matter of debt settlements Great Britain has had very shabby treatment; and had Britain been the creditor, and the United States, France and Italy the debtors, I should have been a little ashamed as a Britisher if we had treated in this fashion a country so closely linked with ours in language, history and race. Perhaps it is unjust to attribute the character of the settlement to the harshness of the American Treasury. It would be fairer to ascribe it to the softness of those who represented our Exchequer. Meanwhile the world has suffered from the blunder and America is not immune.

CHAPTER X

No PERMANENT settlement of the financial problems of Europe is possible without the willing co-operation of the United States. Equally it is true that no return to assured prosperity is possible for the United States until the financial problems of Europe have been satisfactorily settled. Her harvest will always be liable to be blighted by a frosty wind from the chilled plains of Europe. Tariffs do not keep off an east wind.

On previous pages I have discussed the circumstances in which Europe became a debtor continent to America, and I have indicated my views as to the degree to which an insistence on settlement of those debts is or is not morally warranted by their history. But here I propose to brush all those historical considerations aside, and look rather to the present situation and the future prospect, estimating them from a purely practical and realistic standpoint.

At the present time war-debts are owed to America by no less than fourteen European nations. The annual instalments of principal and interest receivable by her in respect of these debts should bring her a yearly income of over 260,000,000 dollars, more than a half of that coming from Britain. The present capital value of these annuities, discounted on a $4\frac{1}{4}$ per cent basis, would be a sum approaching a total of 7,000,000,000 dollars.

It is quite easy to understand the horror which is aroused in the United States when it is suggested that such a debt should be cancelled.

REPARATIONS AND WAR-DEBTS

But there is another side to the picture.

In the first place, while these debts were incurred at a time of very high prices, and were funded while prices were still high—though not quite so high—the recent fall in prices has had the effect of increasing immensely the real size of the debts. Speaking of the last reparation settlement, the Basle Committee says in its report:

"Since the Young Plan came into effect, not only has the trade of the world shrunk in volume, but the very exceptional fall in gold prices that has occurred in the last two years has itself added greatly to the real burden, not only of German annuities, but of all payments fixed in gold."

Roundly it may be said that this fall in prices has increased the real value of the debts due to the United States—measured in terms of the purchasing power of the moneys due—by 50 per cent. Half as much again in goods must be handed over by the debtor to pay the same amount in dollars. With regard to the British debt, the fact that we are no longer on the gold standard means a still further addition to our liability, for as our debt is payable in dollars, we have not only to bear the increase in our liability caused by fall of wholesale prices, but the further increase representing the fall of sterling on the exchange, compared with the dollar— a fall which adds nearly a fresh 50 per cent to the already swollen debt.

In the second place, there is no use in shutting one's eyes to the fact that the majority of these debts are now bad. I have pointed out that their payment has hitherto depended on the yield of German reparations. That source is now pumped dry. To start it afresh you would not only have to put a little water in, you would have to continue pouring in more than you get out. That has been the experience of the

123

Dawes pump and of the Young improvement upon it. The next patent pump will be just as great a failure. The whole history of the reparation question has shown that the effort to extract these large international payments on war account leads to an ever-dwindling yield and the bankruptcy of the debtor country. If America insists successfully on the continuance of payment by her continental debtors, despite the fact that they have no reparation receipts to pay with, she will only bring about in their case a repetition of a similar experience of diminishing returns, defaults, and ultimate bankruptcy. Setting aside altogether the moral aspect of such a proceeding, it is obvious that if she drives her late associates in the World War into insolvency she is bankrupting her best customers.

In the third place, it is worth while to ask what price America is now paying for the receipts she has obtained in the past from her war debtors, and for her expectation of renewed payments in the future. It is possible to buy dollars too dear.

The story of these international payments which I have briefly outlined in previous chapters demonstrates beyond question how immediately they are connected, as cause to effect, with the world-wide slump of industry and finance which is now afflicting all countries to a greater or less extent, and manifesting its worst symptoms in Germany and the United States—the two countries which occupy extreme positions as the principal debtor and the principal creditor in respect of war liabilities.

To people living in the heart of the American continent, Europe may seem a great distance away, and its troubles relatively unimportant. But the distance is not great enough to prevent Europe's economic chaos from ruining the price which the American farmer can hope to get for his wheat, or the American plantation-owner for his cotton. The troubles of Europe are filling the streets of American cities with unemployed and its courts with bankrupts.

Directly and indirectly, through loss of trade with debtor countries, through collapse of prices of her products, through depreciation of value in her securities and investments, through the cost of unemployment, bank failures and shattered industries, America is now losing far more through this world-wide depression that war-debts have induced than the payment of those debts can possibly compensate her.

The total national income of the population of the United States was estimated in 1929 to be 90,000,000,000 dollars. A recent estimate puts the amount by which this national income had declined in 1931 at 20,000,000,000 dollars. At this rate America has lost in a single year three times as much as the whole capital value of the war-debts due to her, and nearly eighty times as much as the total of one year's annuities.

Even if we assess the unemployment in the United States during 1931 at the very conservative figure of 6,000,000, this would imply a decline in the national income of at least 10,000,000,000 dollars. To this must be added the millions who are only partly employed and thus only earn half wages. The actual decline in the earnings of the workers alone will thus be found to be not far from the higher estimate already quoted of the total reduction in the national income.

The estimated yield of income tax in the United States for 1931–2 is 1,259,000,000 dollars below that of 1929–30. This means a loss to the Exchequer on this count alone of nearly five times the amount which the debt annuities would contribute. The anticipated deficit in the Federal budget has been estimated at 2,123,000,000 dollars. The decline in value of United States exports of merchandise in 1931 from the level of 1930 was 1,417,000,000 dollars; compared with the exports of 1929, the decline was twice as great. About 2,000 banks failed in the United States during 1931, the deposits in these banks amounting to 1,500,000,000 dollars. The fall in iron and steel production in the United States in 1931, compared with 1929, was greater than the corresponding fall in all the rest of the world put together.

There has been a catastrophic fall in the market value of American securities and properties. That may not, however, be altogether irretrievable, as a world recovery from the present depression would send up these values once more, not to sky-scraping heights but to more accessible levels. But the present losses being suffered year by year by the American people in trade, employment and income are real, immediate and undeniable.

Nor is there any present sign of improvement. In January 1932, production, export trade, transport, security values, bank clearings, retail business had all shown a further fall from the level of the previous month, and an immense decline as compared with January 1931. A letter written to me in January 1932 by a friend in the States who has had excellent opportunities of observing the condition of things there, contains the following harrowing account of present conditions in that wealthy country:

"There is one word which describes the whole feeling in America to-day, and that is *disillusionment:* disillusionment in the leaders, disillusionment in the business men, disillusionment in politics, disillusionment in prohibition—and even the gangsters have lost their glamour. The greatest disillusionment, however, is that of the worker, who only two years ago was getting £8, £10, £12 a week, and now has to stand in the bread line. I had last night a vivid picture of the contrast of the America of yesterday with the America of to-day, when I strolled down the most dazzling part of Broadway. Piccadilly would be like a Methodist chapel in

126

the country compared with the electric lights and the movies and the dance places there. But right in the centre I saw hundreds and hundreds of poor fellows in single file, some of them in clothes which once were good, all waiting to be handed out two sandwiches, a doughnut, a cup of coffee and a cigarette. I expect a large percentage of them had their own car a couple of years ago. They now seemed jolly glad to get a bite to eat.

"What a crash there has been can be seen from the following figures. Take steel production. Only last March it was 57 per cent of capacity. The figures of last March seem high when you consider that in the end of December steel production was down to 22 per cent! With many hundreds of thousands directly, and millions indirectly, dependent upon this staple industry, it is easy to realize the suffering entailed. United States Steel and Bethlehem cut wages 10 per cent last October; but the cut is really much worse, because most men only work a day or two or a few afternoons.

"Since the middle of 1929, business has fallen from 11 per cent above normal to 44 per cent below normal.

"In the same period common stock prices have fallen more than 75 per cent, and wholesale commodity prices more than 30 per cent. The liquidation spread to the bond market, and here prices have dropped 20 per cent. This has its effects on the banking situation. In 1931 more than 2,000 commercial banks failed in America. . . .

"The towns seem to be heading for bankruptcy. Chicago, of course, is bankrupt. On January 12th it was estimated that 7,000 teachers in Chicago went without lunch. They were hungry because they could not afford even soup and a roll. They have only received pay for six weeks in the last seven months they have taught. Thousands of policemen, firemen, librarians, truck drivers, inspectors, and other municipal employees are in a precarious plight. The city of Chicago,

127

with 200,000,000,000 dollars of tangible wealth, cannot afford to pay them, and is thinking of closing the schools. Philadelphia and Detroit are in almost as bad a situation. And New York is now heading that way. In Detroit the teachers are expecting not to be paid. The pay of the civil servants in Philadelphia has been postponed. Tammany has stopped giving out money and food, and New York City will have to make drastic cuts in poor relief if it is to escape bankruptcy. The city government has had to cut down numberless projects already. 'I expect bread riots!' said a Wall Street man to me yesterday. Bread riots in the richest city in the world!"

America ought not to misunderstand the nature of the European plea for cancellation of all war-debts, including reparations. Europe is not suing America *in forma pauperis*. Britain certainly has never done so, and is not in the least disposed to do so now. She is in respect of war-debts more a creditor country than a debtor, with a substantial balance in her favour. But she has been and still is the largest international trader, and knows the folly and danger, from the standpoint of world business, of keeping alive these debts incurred for no value received. Her attitude is dictated by that common sense which knows when it is wise to be magnanimous.

America is the largest—but not so much the largest—war creditor. Has she not found out that she is not immune from the perils which have afflicted the trade of Britain, and that these perils are intensified if not created by combining an insistence on payment of debts with the exclusion at the same time of all the goods whereby alone they can be paid? Let America believe that when Europe pleads for cancellation, it is not the appeal of a shifty debtor who is whining for mercy. Europe has paid until American banks are gorged with her gold, and Germany especially has made such efforts to pay that she is staggering at her bench from sheer exhaustion. France is putting forward no plea. She is quite content to let her debts be paid for her by her ancient enemy. Her theory is that it keeps the Germans out of mischief, and that anyhow they thoroughly deserve the trouble they are in because of the greater trouble they have wrought.

America holds the key of the gateway which leads to prosperity, for herself as well as for the world. Britain has already surrendered her keys. The Hoover moratorium was a forward step toward that gateway, but it stopped short of a final opening of the road. It delayed the threatened crash in Central Europe, but it has not averted it. No one knows what will happen when the moratorium lapses. The uncertainty paralyzes enterprise. Industry and finance are afraid of moving forward lest they be overwhelmed by the crazy edifice, when its temporary props are withdrawn.

America had better make up her mind soon—as soon as the presidential election is over—to make the best of a bad job, bearing in mind the wise words that the Secretary of the American Treasury uttered years ago in his Debt Commission Report:

"The entire foreign debt is not worth as much to the American people in dollars and cents as a prosperous Europe as a customer."

Europe cannot pay unless America takes her goods. If America cannot in her own interests take payment in goods—and she must be the sole judge of that—then Europe has no other means of paying, for her gold is already shared between America and France. If America follows the wise example of a country older in the ways of international commerce than herself, and agrees to cancellation, she will by cutting her loss ensure a greater gain. She must know by now that she can no more keep out European bankruptcy from invading her fields and factories than she can keep the wind from sweeping across the Atlantic from the shores of Europe, over her highest barriers and through imperceptible crevices into her most carefully constructed shelters.

It is no use saying, "Let Europe go to perdition!" The last war proved that if Europe goes there, it will in the end drag America along. Twelve years of peace have furnished another illustration of the same inevitable truth. That is why no thoughtful American can say, "Ring down the fire-curtain, and let Europe burn to ashes!" Ashes cannot pay debts; neither can ashes buy cotton, wheat, or copper. But America knows now that sparks from a European conflagration can cross the ocean. Indeed, they have already crossed, and the fire is still blazing there. Wall Street is a spectacle of blackened beams, and many an industry farther west exhibits skeletons of twisted girders. That is due to the fire which started in Europe; and the cellared riches that poured in from the depleted stores of Europe have only added fuel to the flames.

There is no country in the world so given to generous impulses as America. And any great impulse in America leads straight to great action. One can never forget how during the war men and women of all classes living in a land of overflowing abundance imposed voluntary restrictions not only on their luxuries but on their plain comforts in order to provide a surplus for distribution amongst the needy population of their Allies in Europe. If America hesitates to-day to crown her honourable mood of sacrifice for humanity in the war by relieving the panting millions of Europe of a burden they agreed in the hour of their agony to carry for American lenders, it is not because the people of the great Republic are greedy, or grasping or mean. It is because they are suspicious of Europe and not without some reason.

REPARATIONS AND WAR-DEBTS

Is it not possible somehow to remove those suspicions when they are legitimate, not by smooth words but by tangible deeds?

International suspicion is the root, not of all evil, but of some of the worst of evils. Nations like dogs are always convinced that the other dog is out to steal their bone and they take elaborate precautions against the fancied calamity, wasting time and energy which would be much more profitably employed in procuring a fresh supply. Much of our world trouble has arisen from national misunderstanding and suspicions, and its perpetuation is due to the same cause. However much man has progressed individually in his social attitude towards his fellowman, internationally he is still in the canine stage. The Founder of the Christian faith answered the question, "Who is my neighbour?" with the reply "He who has fallen amongst thieves." Modern Nationalism answering the question, "Who are my neighbours?" would respond, "They who would fall on my country like thieves." That is the explanation of these Chinese walls of armaments and tariffs. Can we do something to dispel these suspicions which like a dense fog are hanging on frontiers and preventing one nation from seeing another as it really is? Until we do so all nations must suffer alike from this blighting weather that keeps back the spring.

America may say to Europe: "While you pretend that you are too poor to pay your debts, you are finding annually a sum of £520,000,000 to maintain and strengthen your colossal armaments. These expensive and destructive pests got you into a horrible mess a few years ago, and you dragged us in. Now you are worse than ever; you are spending more each year on incendiary bombs. If we forgive your debts you will spend still more. Cut down those threatening and dangerous machines for human slaughter! Then we will reconsider the situation."

REPARATIONS AND WAR-DEBTS

That would be quite a reasonable attitude to take up; although it is not quite the same thing, as I have pointed out, to spend money, even foolishly, inside a country in its own currency as to transmit it to another country in the currency which would be accepted there. All the same, armaments are a menacing and hazardous expenditure, and it would be a service to humanity if America made the fullest use of her dominant financial position to enforce such a reduction as would render them harmless.

CHAPTER XI

AN INTERNATIONAL conference was to have assembled at Lausanne in February of this year to consider the international financial situation, with special reference to reparations. It was postponed, but is now promised us in the summer.

The delay is particularly unfortunate in view of the warning sounded by the Basle Committee in their report that no delay should be permitted "in coming to decisions which will bring an amelioration of this grave crisis which weighs so heavily on all alike." On June 30th the Hoover moratorium expires. There is at present no faintest prospect that the continent of Europe will then be in a position to resume payment in respect of its international war liabilities. Indeed, the Basle Committee have already reported in favour of postponement of the postponable reparation annuities, thus cutting off the source of supply for the bulk of war-debt payments. And there is scant reason to hope that even the non-postponable annuities will by then be forthcoming from Germany.

It is no use floating helplessly down to catastrophe on a Micawber stream of hope that something will turn up to save the situation. Obviously some agreement must be reached before midsummer between the responsible Powers that will prevent the moratorium expiring until their conference has evolved a satisfactory plan to deal with the situation. Obviously, too, it is worse than futile to think of merely postponing the issue from month to month by extensions of the existing moratoria on war liabilities and on the short-term loans that have been granted to Central Europe. Financial recovery is impossible under such conditions. There is nowhere any firm foundation on which industry and commerce can begin to reconstruct their activities. Trade may for the time being be keeping off the quicksands, but it is not getting on. It is not leaving the quagmire behind altogether, and travelling along the firmer ground beyond.

In the light of the conclusions of the Basle Committee, reinforcing as they do the pronouncements of the committee which examined the situation in August at the request of the Bank for International Settlements, it is no longer possible to deny or ignore the financial exhaustion of Germany. Play is made in some quarters with the fact that by her post-war currency inflation Germany wiped out her internal debt, and that in consequence the *per capita* debt now resting on her people is much lighter than in some of the victorious countries. But such an argument overlooks the fact that this process, far from reflecting any growth of Germany's national wealth, was in fact a source of further impoverishment. True, it destroyed the internal debt of the Reich and the provinces to their nationals, but at the same time it destroyed the value of bonds, debentures, and of savings in the banks, and while ruining the rentier classes it also destroyed the credit and working capital essential to finance industrial and commercial development. In Germany to-day the smallness of the *per capita* debt reflects the fact that the Government is so impoverished as to be almost without credit; and the destruction of internal working capital through inflation has compelled both the German Government and German industries to apply to foreign sources for loans to keep them going, so that a very large part of German indebtedness to-day, instead of completing its circle of payments within the country—as is the case with our internal debt—is a liability to foreign creditors, and a load on its external balance of payments.

I have touched on this aspect of Germany's financial position because it in fact supplies an additional proof of her grave plight, and of the folly of building high hopes of large subventions from her in the near future. Pressure on her which resulted in her renewed bankruptcy would not now so much ruin her rentiers—they have already been ruined—as it would ruin the bankers and investors of other countries who have since her inflationary collapse been supplying her with credits and funds for her rehabilitation.

It would also be stupid to ignore the political position in Germany. The present chancellor, Herr Brüning, represents moderate and pacific opinion in that great country. And yet he has been driven in order to save the country from the tightening grip of revolutionary movements, which are clutching at the arms of the Fatherland from the right and the left, to declare unequivocally that Germany can no longer pay reparation annuities. There is widespread privation and despair throughout the land. It is true that Germany is not the only country that is enduring hunger through unemployment. But in Germany politicians are saying, and not without a show of reason, that the suffering has been brought upon the country by the bondage of the Treaty. There is not a German who does not believe it, and no government founded, as a democracy must be, on the will of the people can exist for a week if it calls upon German traders, manufacturers and workers to make further sacrifices for reparations. It is no use talking about the sacredness of contracts. The Allies have already discredited that plea by their shameless refusal to carry out their part of it. The defeat of Hitlerism and Communism at the coming presidential election will not, therefore, mean the resurrection of the Young annuities. It will only mean that the language of

135

refusal will be more diplomatic and that the tone of negation will be more subdued. A democratic government cannot pay and a nationalist or communist dictatorship would not pay. Another Ruhr invasion is inconceivable. It is not so much that Europe and America in their present state of nervelessness will stand anything from the Yangtze to the Rhine. It is more than that. It is a conviction born of experience that a hammer cannot extract blood out of a stone. The troops would not be furnished from the editorial staffs of Chauvinistic papers. The bitterest of their writers never fought. They would have to come from the villages, the mines and the factories, and the French peasant and ouvrier are fed up with the kind of swagger which has already robbed them of four-fifths of their savings under the guise of stabilizing them and has produced worse unemployment in France than this generation has ever seen.

In facing the future, therefore, we must definitely accommodate ourselves to the prospect of no further contributions from Germany except, at the best, the service of the loans she has already incurred, including the Dawes and Young loans on reparation account. Consideration of the problem of war-debts owing between the victors of the World War must proceed from this basis.

I am quite convinced of the disconcerting fact that this is not a specially good time for making an appeal to the sanity that transcends patriotism. In the democratic countries of the world we are passing through a period of elections which will determine the policy of these countries for years to come, and it is unfortunate that the rampageous nationalism which has been responsible for a good deal, if not most, of our present trouble from 1914 onwards is raging more virulently than ever at this hour. For that reason, at all these elections party goods in order to sell have to be wrapped up in the gaudiest colours of the national flag. Neither the quality nor quantity counts: it is only the wrapping that matters. Britain has just gone through her elections with a cry of shutting out the foreigner. In America there is, I understand, much irrelevant talk about America for the Americans, and a 100 per cent Americanism.

It is clear that an appeal of the same character is to be addressed to the French public at the coming election: in Japan there was but one appeal, "Vindicate Japanese rights," and at the coming presidential elections in Germany the cry will be, "Save the Fatherland from the fangs of the Treaty."

In the present temper of the world the dropped portcullis and the raised drawbridge are the national emblems in every State. From the short-sighted point of view something might have been said for these policies, had they not already been tried in every country in the world and brought ruin to every one of them in turn. The richest countries have been hit as hard as the poorest by this policy of exclusiveness. Selfishness is a depreciating currency. You may cash it at its full face value at first, but if you watch the exchanges for some time, you will find it always sags in the end. "Am I my brother's keeper?" may get a man or a nation out of a temporary embarrassment, but in the long run they find that it is not only inhuman, but bad business for themselves. A British government understood the commercial aspect of this truth ten years ago. They realized that although the nominal value of the debts due from foreign countries to Britain was prodigious, and that if collected our bank cellars would be fabulously enriched, the indirect damage done to international trade would be so great that Britain would on balance be a heavy loser. Is it hopeless to bring this home to the mind as well as the heart of commercial and industrial and agricultural America?

Hitherto America has stood out rigidly for payment of the

war-debts owed to her. Payment was made up to the inter-
vention of the Hoover moratorium. Mainly it came in gold—
and the mass of the people of the United States are no better
off for the fact that somewhere there are bank vaults stuffed
with bars of gold, that can be neither eaten nor used for any
serviceable production; whilst they are very much worse off
for the fact that their wheat and cotton fetch bankrupt stock
prices, and that their customers throughout the world cannot
afford to buy their goods. For America, a measure of all-
round cancellation would be extremely good business.

France also is a country with views that stand in the way
of general cancellation. Not only is France the biggest
recipient of reparations, and after America the biggest net
recipient on balance in respect of international war liabilities
—thanks to the large measure of debt cancellation she was
granted both by us and by the United States—but she is also
desperately afraid of anything which might impair the
sanctity of the Treaty of Versailles, and the existing partition
and settlement of Europe which was established by that
treaty. She knows that powerful forces are gathering to urge
revision of the Treaty in certain of its aspects, and she fears
lest cancellation of reparations should prove the first breach,
and a precedent for further attacks.

Although I took a leading part in the framing of the
Treaty, I do not claim on that account that I have the right
to speak with any special authority on the interpretation. But
I assert as clearly as possible my view that in present circumstances an agreement to cancel future reparation payments
from Germany would not be a breach of the sanctity of the
Treaty of Versailles. It would on the contrary be the truest
way to administer and honour it. In supporting this conten-
tion I refer the reader to Clause 234 of the Treaty, which I
have already quoted at full length.*

*See Chapter IV, pages 24–25.

REPARATIONS AND WAR-DEBTS

The Treaty only laid it down that Germany must make good the damage wrought, up to the limit of her capacity—not beyond it; and it made provision whereby this capacity could be assessed from time to time, and any part of the charges laid on Germany cancelled, by agreement among the Powers affected. When we speak of the sanctity of the Treaty, we must apply this not only to the sanctity of the provision that Germany must pay all she can, but no less to the sanctity of those provisions designed to ensure that her capacity to pay was fairly measured, and the demands on her limited accordingly. To drive Germany to bankruptcy in a vain effort to get more than she can pay is not to honour the Treaty, but not only to break it, but to dishonour it.

If it would be good business for the United States to agree to all-round cancellation, it is for France both good business and good law.

It may be added that France is the last country that should stand on a punctilio about the Treaty of Versailles. What about armaments; and the pledge implicit in the Treaty that German disarmament should be followed and paralleled by her own? Yet France has to-day an army, with reserves, of over five millions, and thousands of heavy guns. No other country in Europe has an armament in any way comparable. Italy, her nearest rival, has stated that she is willing to reduce her armaments on any scale generally agreed by the Powers. Germany has an army of only 100,000 men, and very few guns or munitions. The immense land armaments of France are a glaring and arrogant breach of the undertakings of Versailles.

Finally, the process of fining down from conference to conference the liability of Germany in respect of reparation annuities has been tried for over eleven years, and has ended in a bewildering chaos. It is no longer worth while to consider whether there might subsequently be a sum of money

139

to be extracted from Germany, for the process of extraction is for the world a process of distraction, taking the mind of statesmanship in Europe and America from other and more important matters. To sit still, waiting for windfalls from reparations and war-debts, instead of getting busy on the restoration of world trade and industry, is a form of conduct as reprehensible as that of a firm which wastes the whole time and energy of its staff in vain efforts to collect stale book debts, instead of devoting its thought and activities to transacting and expanding its business.

Opinion is gathering force throughout the world in favour of the wiser policy. In mid-January, Signor Mussolini issued a plea for the "clean slate"; and at the end of the same month Mr. Ramsay MacDonald declared that the policy of this country with regard to reparations and war-debts was "to return to economic sanity and wipe all that out." Bankers, business men, economists, and other responsible leaders of thought in many countries are rallying to the same view. A frank and intelligent examination of the facts will inevitably lead to the general adoption of this attitude.

I conclude, then, by submitting the following propositions, as a summary of the present situation, and of the steps necessary to deal with it:

First: the payment in full of reparations and war-debts, on the scale obtaining up to the operation of the Hoover moratorium last July, cannot be resumed when that moratorium expires, nor within any predictable period thereafter. That schedule has definitely and permanently broken down.

Secondly: the retention of these debts as pending liabilities, to be required in whole or part from the debtor nations at some future date, would in the self-interest of the creditor countries be a piece of very bad business. It would cost them vastly more in loss of trade, unemployment and industrial depression than they could possibly recover under their claims.

Thirdly: for nations which share in modern industrial civilization, with the international commerce it involves, there is a severe limit to the amount which they can profitably exact from another country in respect of war liabilities incurred for no value received. If this limit be passed, further exactions only bring loss to the creditor country.

Fourthly: while it would be a commercially sound business proceeding to wipe out these debts, it would also have moral and legal warrant—as to war-debts, in view of the circumstances in which they were contracted; and as to reparations, in view of the conditions in the Treaty of Versailles to which their exaction is subject.

Fifthly: in view of the fact that these liabilities arose out of war operations, any measure of cancellation offered should be subject to acceptance and fulfilment by the debtor nations of substantial measures of disarmament, not only as a warrant of good faith but as a guarantee against further outbreaks which would land the world in a worse plight than it is in at present.

Sixthly: even the complete abolition of all these hampering debts is unlikely by itself to ensure a full reversal of the present tide of depression, unless there is also a breaking away from the policy of economic nationalism which the existence of these international payments has fostered, and a general lowering of tariff barriers and resumption of full and vigorous international commerce.

Seventhly: it is vital that the nations concerned with these issues should arrive at agreement with the least possible delay on a permanent and constructive policy to deal with them. At this juncture, playing for time is not playing for safety, but fooling with the accelerator whilst the car is rushing down hill. The whole machinery of the existing economic order is at stake. If it crashes it will not be worth picking up as scrap iron. It is no time for nerveless vagueness and diplomatic hesitancy. Democracies are not nearly as timid as their leaders. The statesmen responsible in each country must boldly make up their minds as to the course of action necessary to deal with the situation, and abandon or brush aside all attempts to quibble, to temporize or to obstruct the prompt carrying out of sound, constructive measures.

I have made it clear that in my own view no measure can have a chance until you clear out of the way this rubble of war ledgers.

THE END

INDEX

143

INDEX

INDEX

INDEX

INDEX

INDEX

INDEX

INDEX